Investor Relations

Investor Relations

~~~

The Art and Philosophy of

Effective Corporate Communications

THOMAS J. LAURIA

Library of Congress Cataloging-in-Publication Data
Lauria, Thomas J., 1969 -
Investor Relations: The Art and Philosophy of
Effective Corporate Communications
/ by Thomas J. Lauria

ISBN - 978-0-557-00763-9

To Mom and Dad, for your love and support.

Favorite Quotes

"Curiosity is such as precious gift which comes so naturally to us that we sometimes fail to appreciate it."

Arno Penzias

Nobel Prize Winner and Bell Labs Scientist Nobel Banquet Speech, December 10, 1978

Arno Penzias, a Bell Labs astrophysicist, is credited with finding evidence that all the galaxies and elements in the universe were created from a massive explosion; evidence which supported the "big bang" theory.

On Success and Accomplishment

"If at first the idea is not absurd, then there is no hope for it."

Albert Einstein

"There's nothing like a couple of wins to put a spring in your step."

Charles Krauthammer

"One of the great discoveries a man makes, one of his great surprises, is to find he can do what he was afraid he couldn't do. Most of the bars we beat against are in ourselves – we put them there, and we can take them down."

Henry Ford

"Success is a lousy teacher. It seduces smart people into thinking they can't lose."

Bill Gates

On Opinion and Belief

"They deem him their worst enemy who tells them the truth."

Plato

"It is the duty of everyone to spread what he believes to be the truth."

Charles Darwin

"If you cannot persuade your colleagues of the correctness of your position, it is probably worthwhile to rethink your own."

Alan Greenspan

Favorite Quotes

On Business Economics, Stock Markets, and Investments

"Never invest in a business you cannot understand."

"If past history was all there was to the game, the richest people would be librarians."

Warren Buffett

"When a management with a reputation for brilliance tackles a business with a reputation for bad economics, it is the reputation of the business that remains intact."

Warren Buffett

"…we slave one hour, we get one white chip for the Game. But three of us form a little company, create stock (paper), earn $50,000, and our public liquid market will give us not $50,000 but a million if we can convince it that the piece of paper is worth twenty times earnings. That is really effortless wealth…"

'Adam Smith'
The Money Game

On Corporate Buyouts

"Fellows, it's got to be seventy-five cash. You can't put paper on the table. It looks low class."

Ross Johnson, former CEO of RJR Nabisco commenting on the need for the company's corporate takeover to made with an all-cash offer. He rebuked a suggestion that it include three dollars of preferred stock.

Barbarians at the Gate

On Thought and Failure

"Thinking is the hardest work there is, which is probably the reason so few engage in it."

"Failure is only the opportunity to begin again more intelligently."

Henry Ford

Important Disclaimer

Contents

Contents

Contents

8. Retail Shareholder Marketing Program, 87

9. Strategic Elements of Investor Relations, 97

Contents

About The Author

Thomas J. Lauria was the senior telecom equipment analyst and director of telecom equipment research at ING Barings LLC. In that capacity, he provided research coverage on telecom equipment companies including Nortel Networks, Lucent Technologies, Cisco Systems, Ciena Corp., and Juniper Networks. His institutional clients included Fidelity Management and Research, Goldman Sachs, Capital Research, Wellington, State Street, Putnam, J.P. Morgan, Credit Suisse, and U.S. Trust.

Prior to joining ING Barings, Mr. Lauria served in the capacity of Investor Relations Director at Lucent Technologies. He held senior positions in Lucent's Investor Relations team from its initial public offering from AT&T in April 1996 until leaving the firm to join ING Barings. While at Lucent, he had responsibility for the company's marketing program to its institutional shareholder base and had extensive relationships with its most influential investors, portfolio managers and financial analysts. Many of the primary relationships formed while at Lucent Technologies and AT&T became trading clients of ING Barings.

After leaving ING Barings, he founded Avtera LLC where he conducts qualitative hedge fund manager research, performance monitoring, and research due diligence primarily on equity long-short managers, emerging managers, and emerging markets managers. He attends prime brokerage capital introductions events, including those of Credit Suisse, UBS, Deutsche Bank, and Lehman Brothers. He is a member of the New York Hedge Fund Roundtable, and has hosted hedge fund meetings with Nobel Laureates Joseph Stiglitz and Edmund Phelps, both of Columbia University. Mr. Lauria is a private investor in alternative investments, large-cap technology stocks, and financial services companies.

As part of Lucent's spin-off from AT&T in 1996, the company's initial public stock offering was the world's largest. During his tenure with Lucent, the company from obscurity to being ranked 22nd on the Fortune 500 list of largest companies; had 153,000 total employee; 5 million shareholders; and reached a staggering market valuation of $280 billion. The company established and rolled out its new corporate brand, while defying the odds and surpassing its former parent company, AT&T, as the most widely held stock in America. Lucent's efforts earned it many awards for outstanding investor relations, including being awarded, Investor Relations Magazine's "Best Investor Relations for an IPO" as well as the prestigious "Gold Quill" award. Over time, Lucent's investor relations team grew from its core base of members to a group of thirteen at its peak. While a large investor relations effort by most standards, it was far below AT&T's twenty members.

While at Lucent, Mr. Lauria was responsible for the company's extensive meetings program, including its extensive road shows program, quarterly earnings reporting process, its trade show outreach initiative, quarterly business unit results meetings, and corporate product handbook. He was the point of contact for the firm with its New York Stock Exchange specialist firm, LaBranch & Company and also managed is internal and external investor survey program. Mr. Lauria developed and wrote the company's quarterly investor relations newsletter, *HighLights*. He routinely oversaw the development of executive presentations and attended many Wall Street conferences with the company's most senior executives and business unit heads. He conducted institutional investor meetings throughout the United States and conducted a European Roadshow with presentations in Europe's largest financial centers, including London, Geneva, Zurich, and Paris.

About The Author

Mr. Lauria has conducted numerous live media segments and has been a regular guest on CNBC's Power Lunch with Maria Bartiromo. He has been regularly interviewed on CNBC, The Nightly Business Report on PBS, Bloomberg television and CNN. In addition, he has been interviewed on live radio programs including CBS Market Watch and Bloomberg radio. He has received extensive print coverage in Reuters, Dow Jones Newswires, *The Wall Street Journal*, *The New York Times* and *TheStreet.com*.

Prior to joining Lucent, he was a strategic marketing manager for Carly Fiorina's AT&T Network Systems Atlantic/Canadian region and was responsible for timely market intelligence of the global telecommunications industry. Mr. Lauria also served as a competitor intelligence manager in AT&T's competitive intelligence and market research organization. In this capacity, he was responsible for analyzing the company's equipment manufacturing competition and its service provider customers. Mr. Lauria received a master's degree in management from the Stevens Institute of Technology, for which he ranked first in academic achievement and received the department's Outstanding Academic Achievement Award. He completed his graduate thesis with Kidder Peabody & Company, where his pro bono research analyzed and optimized the firm's quantitative asset allocation (stock/bond/cash) models and compared them to those of other major financial institutions.

Mr. Lauria received his bachelor's degree in mechanical engineering with honors, also from Stevens Institute of Technology. He attended the Emerging Leader Development Program of Columbia University's graduate school of business, the Leadership Continuity Program with AT&T and Lucent, including coursework at George Washington University, and attended an advanced program at The Brookings Institution Center for Public Policy Education, Washington, D.C. He was granted two U.S. Patents in technology. He is the author of, *The Fall of Telecom: A Wall Street Analyst's True Story of The Telecom Industry*. The host of CNBC's *Kudlow & Co.*, Lawrence C. Kudlow, authored the book's foreword. Mr. Kudlow was the chief U.S. economist at ING Barings.

Preface

The primary objective of this handbook is to create a comprehensive knowledge base on the broad and sometimes misunderstood topic of investor relations, the center of most corporate communications programs. The approach taken was to first develop a thorough understanding of Wall Street itself, the Investor Relations Officer's (IRO) most visible constituency. It is not uncommon for many corporate IROs to misunderstand the daily activities and responsibilities of Wall Street analysts and institutional investors, their primary clients. As a result, many IROs on Main Street tend to misunderstand the needs of these important constituents.

Having been a Fortune 25 corporate Investor Relations Director as well as a Sr. Equity Analyst and Equity Research Director, the perception of what is needed by the financial community is quite different than what many investor relations officers believe. However, by providing a thorough understanding of Wall Street itself, a solid foundation of knowledge as to what the role entails will become a strong basis for implementing and structuring an effective investor communication program.

While on the surface Wall Street analysts and institutional investors are the primary, if not only, constituencies served by the IRO, that perception is far from the case in actuality. The number of internal constituencies served is numerous, and range from being a

Preface

public relations (PR) coordinator to being a sounding board for corporate business development initiatives and advisor to senior management. Serving these various constituencies requires great consumptions in time. As a result, many spend approximately half of their time dealing with external clients and the other half managing internal clients and responsibilities.

Of course, all publicly traded companies perform the function of Investor Relations (IR), whether or not they are large multi-billion dollar corporations, corporate spin-offs or even the countless smaller companies that conducted initial public offerings (IPOs) in the heyday of Wall Street's famed bull market in the mid- to late- 1990s. Accordingly, IR programs must be tailored to the company's resources and while smaller companies are more resource constrained, *all IR programs* can be both effective and of high quality. It would not be accurate for one to believe that only large companies have the necessary resources to manage an effective communications program, as many smaller public companies often drive highly efficient investor communications efforts.

Driving a "hyperactive" Investor Relations program is the ultimate aim of this text. The author believes that the insight provided herein will enable new IROs to best understand their new profession and enable existing practitioners to add additional elements to their marketing programs that will enhance shareholder understanding and value. Investor Relations is where Main Street meets Wall Street and the waters are pretty rough on both sides of the River. It is a pleasure to share with you my views on this topic and hope that you find this handbook both interesting and informative. Please visit my website at www.tomlauria.com for more information.

Thomas J. Lauria

1

Investor Relations

Within all public corporations, regardless of their size, the function of Investor Relations plays a critical role within the company. Most corporate members of both senior management, as well as rank and file employees, are highly interested in Wall Street's opinion of the company, its competition, customers and the overall dynamics of the marketplace. For this reason alone, management will often consult with the Investor Relations Officer for an opinion on how various corporate decisions and strategies are likely to be received by the investment community before making final decisions.

Management's high level of interest in Wall Street's opinions and the opinion of the IRO is largely predicated on the corporation's responsibility to effectively communicate with its owners and to protect shareholder value. Naturally, senior management may also have a desire to protect their own financial interest in the corporation, which is often in the form of stock options, directly-held shares, equity warrants, performance incentives and cash or stock bonuses. In some cases, management performance incentives may be partially linked to the company's improvement in or attainment of certain key financial metrics. Members of the management team often have a keen desire to understand the complex demands of Wall Street, to be in the Street's inner circle and to maintain positions of power within the company. With a solid understanding of Wall Street, members of corporate management can be viewed very positively by their board of directors, peers, the investment community itself and even by the media. Being tuned into this inner circle of influence is often the key to acquiring and maintaining corporate power.

But as an Investor Relations Officer, given the frequency of your interactions with the financial community, you may be viewed as a proxy for Wall Street in the minds of the management team. Likewise, given the frequency of your interactions with senior management, to the investment community, you are a proxy for the company. Hence, as an IRO your opinion is quite an important one and the power you have both inside and outside the company is greater than you may realize and your position of power and influence often remains unchallenged.

Selecting an IRO and Establishing Credibility With The Street

To most members of the financial community, their Investor Relations contact essentially *is* the company and having someone in the Investor Relations role that has credibility as an honest and trustworthy spokesperson is absolutely critical. While having a finance background is essential, other skills are clearly necessary for an IRO to be effective. Those individuals that prefer the comfort of accounting and an Excel spreadsheet will soon find themselves outside their comfort zone discussing the nuances of recent corporate acquisitions, product details, patent expiration dates and marketing strategies. In addition to assisting analysts with their understanding of the company, their financial expectations and differentiating factors versus its nearest competitors, the IRO will also be highly involved in briefing management members for upcoming road shows and investor visits, reviewing prepared management talking points and even writing or assisting their public relations (PR) counterparts with drafting conference call scripts, press releases and talking points.

The head of IR acts as a bridge between senior management and the investment community, and hence the role is most certainly a combination of effective finance, marketing and public relations skills.

The diverse expertise and credibility necessary for an IRO to be truly effective requires careful selection by senior management.

While the unique balance of acquired expertise and natural skill set make some IROs career practitioners of the trade, many companies utilize the position of Investor Relations Vice President as a rotational position, typically for about two years. In that way, on their way up the corporate ladder, the rotational IR Vice President will understand Wall Street, the demands and expectations of the financial community and be able to apply that knowledge in the various management positions that follow. The rotational IRO will have an opportunity to see the company from a very unique vantage point and uniquely observe the company's place in the industry, particularly in relation to its competitors.

While there are clearly benefits to rotating IROs every few years to prepare them for senior management roles - and their future interactions with Wall Street - the function itself is a highly specialized one. As such, being a good practitioner requires an intangible element that is generally acquired after the normal two-year rotational period has concluded. In order to be fully respected by Wall Street clients, an effective IRO must not only be firmly rooted in the practice and nuances of Investor Relations but also have a firm handle on the company's market, business lines and even its competition. Otherwise, the IRO may be viewed negatively by the financial community and can be a detriment to the company and its hard-earned reputation.

With the pace of learning that occurs throughout an IRO's tenure being truly remarkable, we encourage senior executives not to consider the IR VP as a two-year rotational position within the company, but rather for a commitment of three to five years. It is important to consider that the responsiveness and knowledge of the IR staff can lead to a high level of respect, trust and credibility between the IRO and its external clients. These factors can become quite important as analysts and investors evaluate corporate data and analyze it against data from other industry sources. As credibility with Wall Street takes time to develop, once achieved it must treated as an asset within the company. As the primary contacts for Wall Street analysts and investors, it is essential to ensure that your Investor Relations program is of the highest quality. Having a highly skilled and seasoned IR team is absolutely critical to earning the respect of the investment community.

The Official Investor Liaison and Numerous Unofficial Roles

As an IR professional, your official role is that of a corporate liaison between senior management and the investment community. The IR department is generally established by the corporation to field the majority of questions from the investment community toward the company. Its formal role is to manage these relationships effectively. In the end, your primary responsibility is to effectively satisfy and manage the needs of the financial community by presenting a fair and accurate description of the company, its market opportunities and competitive product and market positioning.

In practice however, the role of the Investor Relations professional is to juggle the demands of its various customer sets. These customers include retail investors (individual shareholders), securities analysts, institutional investors and portfolio managers and senior management. Additionally, IR interfaces quite often with the company's legal counsel, its internal finance organizations (the CFO, unit CFOs, and external reporting groups), as well as the company's Public Relations, Marketing and Business Development teams. At an average corporation, I estimate that approximately half of IRO time will be spent internally. However, IROs of very large corporations may spend most of their time internally and delegate many external responsibilities to their capable support staffs.

The IRO, As Analyst

With so many hats being worn, it is critical that the IRO develop and possess high levels of knowledge about the company, its history, products, industry and competition. In many ways, a good IRO is also an effective analyst – focusing keenly on the results of the company's competitors. Knowledge of the firm's competition, recent product introductions, management changes, corporate acquisitions and other industry developments are key to representing the IRO's company accurately. In this way, the IRO gains the respect of the financial community and is more than an astute and guarded corporate representative and keeper of the company's ongoing financial results and guidance.

In my view, it is often reasonable and helpful for an IRO to discuss the broader industry with the financial community. As a matter of course, the analyst community will appreciate the insights that your corporate vantage point provides and vice versa. The insight gained by the IRO is often quite interesting and useful to the company's senior management. Accordingly, I encourage all IROs to allocate ample time to understanding macro industry issues and provide management the benefit of notable insights.

The IRO, As Strategic Business Development Partner

Many senior managers and business development directors are particularly interested in the views of analysts, including their reaction to potential M&A activity. While members of the IR team would never discuss specific M&A scenarios with members of the investment community, the financial community creates vast amounts of detailed industry research and analysis, articulating gaps in product portfolios, desirable distribution partnerships, and other strategic issues of value to most business development efforts.

Analysts typically volunteer their opinions on the company and its strategic issues to their Investor Relations counterparts. These viewpoints can be quite insightful to the company's senior management, business development team and corporate strategic planners. As a result, IROs may find themselves as strategic partners with corporate groups, providing insight into areas of strategic interest.

During the business development cycle of an acquisition, Investor Relations may be engaged early on for their views on Wall Street's likely reaction to the acquisition, to help with strategic positioning and to determine the necessary IR efforts and meetings that will be required to adequately support the upcoming announcement. Often, IR interaction occurs much later in the process and when an external announcement is imminent. With regard to business development initiatives, members of IR team work closely with internal groups in relation to details of the announcement, and final terms of the deal, and the timing of necessary regulatory approvals, including meeting the provisions of the Hart Scott Rodino Act and any necessary rules and laws governing fair and adequate disclosure.

Once management decides and the board approves a material and significant acquisition, on the day of the announcement the company will likely host a conference call with the investment community to discuss merger details. On very rare occasions, the company will hold a full-court press conference on short notice to maximize publicity for a major announcement, although the benefits of holding a press conference are not often greater than simply holding an investor/media conference call with real-time web cast. In some cases, the announcement is so significant that employees are gathered to hear and discuss the news.

The IRO, As Public Relations Coordinator

IR is often aware of, but not in a leadership role, with respect to coordinating external public relations efforts and internal employee communications events. Major public relations announcements can be quite involved and elaborate, such as linking corporate executives in various locations by satellite for an all employee broadcast, followed by separate events for investors and the media alike.

The IRO is generally responsible for the majority of the communication between the company and the financial community. While the company's public relations staff generally is responsible for development of day-to-day press releases, IR is often consulted on many of announcements before being finalized. Major announcements are often distributed to the financial community with blast faxes, emails, outbound telephone calls, and blast voicemails as well as publication over the analyst First Call network.

Having a "funnel" or "drumbeat" of upcoming press releases slated for release often proves useful for IR distribution purposes – and also limits the risk of being surprised by the issuance of corporate press releases. While such snafus happen rather infrequently, if a regional PR manager is not in close communication with headquarters, a press release may be issued regionally without fully understanding its impact on corporate messages and themes that are being communicated by senior management. Closely following the upcoming PR "drumbeat" enables the IR team to accurately understand the nuances of each announcement and prepare appropriate investor communications. While being surprised by a press release may not seem probable, in large companies it can happen occasionally – and does.

On a quarterly basis, large companies can issue over a hundred releases. As Wall Street analysts typically follow many companies at a given time, many of then informally, the investment community quickly assesses which press releases are truly news worthy and material and those that are considered merely clutter or "noise." By following their industries closely, Wall Street analysts can quite easily see through the noise and focus their attention on material events. Many companies would be wise to eliminate the volumes of press releases disseminated to the trade press and focus on those that are insightful and truly material to the business.

The Investment Community, Ardent Students of "Body Language"

It is important that the IRO be keenly aware of the their importance and stature in the financial community. As such, their words and body language receive a great deal of observation and scrutiny. With continuous and unobstructed access to the company's senior management, insider knowledge about the company's financials, outlook and strategy, the IRO will generally receive the same level of body language scrutiny that senior executives receive.

Investors will often find themselves reading both good and bad connotations into subtle changes in the frequency of your external communications, the specific words selected in response to the same questions posed to you quarter after quarter, even changes in your voice pattern or energy level. Any changes or observations perceived by the investment community may lead investors to postulate that something is good or bad with the company itself, maybe even based simply on how happy or even tired you appear. It is not unheard of for an IRO to be questioned as to why he or she may seem happier or less energetic than usual. Always attune to body language, institutional investors may even notice the time it takes the IRO to return telephone calls, particularly late in the quarter and to the frequency of outbound calls. Institutional investors may often contact multiple members of the IR team on similar issues, and they are certain to comparing notes in how each member of the IR team responds. They will listen for anything that seems out of the norm.

Whenever management or IR members make public appearances, they are being observed by a devoted group of highly observant and intelligent constituents. Taking center stage publicly can prompt investor questions about the IRO's confidence in the company's annual financial guidance, the likelihood of winning or losing a contract or the perceived need for a partnership or alliance. The spotlight and level of scrutiny may intensify when these public appearances take place in the middle or later part of the quarter, when the quarter's result's are closer to being finalized and management likely knows the results of two out of three months worth of quarterly data. Public appearances and routine conversations in the later part of the quarter generally involve an "all eyes, all ears" critique of body language, tone and word selection. As an IRO, it is important to be highly mindful of your body language.

The Impact of Management's Philosophy Toward Wall Street

The support of senior management is critical to your effectiveness as an Investor Relations Officer. There is no question that each company has its own, unique philosophy on the importance of the Investor Relations program. Consistently strong financial performance has been the traditional hallmark of such companies as General Electric and technology bell whether Cisco Systems. As an example, Cisco has an extremely well-regarded IR program. The company's management team, at many levels, is actively engaged in supporting the program.

At many public companies, quarterly conference calls focus on simply the facts, as presented by the company's CEO and CFO. In essence they focus on what happened during the quarter and what the outlook is for the next quarter and remainder of the fiscal year. In my opinion, Cisco goes above and beyond this level of baseline insight and provides a more detailed quarterly review. In my time covering the company, Cisco routinely articulated additional and detailed progress toward goals and stretch objectives, putting the quarter's results in the context of corporate goals that were reiterated or modified on each quarterly conference call. Moreover the company discussed what was better and worse than expected during the quarter and generally took the opportunity to present a detailed look at a particular area of the company's business. The result was the call was more educational in nature, rather than just a discussion about the quarterly results and business outlook. After the prepared remarks typically concluded, the company has an extensive question and answer session, so extensive in fact that some participants would complain that conference call lasted too long. Cisco holds a long-standing practice of seemingly exhausting all questions from the investment community and thus satisfying their needs, even if a few complaints about the length of the call result.

Conversely, at one time in its vast history, long ago, AT&T held quarterly conference calls but did not have an open question and answer session after management's prepared remarks. As a result, analysts had little opportunity to ask questions on the call. The conference call was held live, but the opportunity for dialogue, questioning and clarification was not present on the large group conference call. Today, some publicly traded companies, particularly very resource-constrained micro-cap firms, do not host quarterly earnings calls. There still remains no requirement by the Securities and Exchange Commission (SEC) requiring public companies to host quarterly conference calls. Rather, the filing of the company's 10Qs, 10Ks and other required filings are the official documents of record.

In my opinion, the golden rule of Investor Relations dictates frequent access and candor as the primary tools to satisfying the needs of the investment community. The more opportunities that the investment community has to ask questions and meet management, the better they will understand the company and the more transparent the company's business will be.

The Golden Rules of Investor Relations: Frequent Access and Candor

I am a firm believer that simply giving investors and analysts access to the company -- even just giving them the mere satisfaction of asking a question -- is a factor in their opinions, and quite possibly valuation, of the company. Some corporations and investors alike believe that a company's market valuation is purely a function of the company's basic financial performance and earnings alone. While certainly a company's financial performance is a primary factor in establishing its market value, the access that investors receive to the company is also a critical influencer to investors' development of a thorough understanding of the company, its market, products, competitive position, opportunities, and challenges.

Historical financials merely state past results while forecasts and beliefs in the future drive share prices and valuations. But without ample and candid access to management – including members of the Investor Relations team – there would be little conviction, understanding and trust behind these forecasts and beliefs in the future. Exhibiting a high level of candor with your investor communications is a critical aspect of developing and maintaining credibility with the investment community.

As a CEO, CFO or Treasurer, the company's annual Investor Relations plan must be adequate based on the company's market cap, financial resources and feedback from the investment community. It is important to drive your Investor Relations effort relentlessly, whether or not your Investor Relations efforts are internally managed or externally so. Accept nothing less than exceedingly high marks for institutional and retail investor satisfaction with your IR program. As members of senior management are focused on operational excellence and driving sales, marketing, manufacturing, and middle management, so too should the same attention be given to ensuring that marketing the company to investors is being performed clearly, articulately, factually, and to your satisfaction.

Never Strive To Convince, But Rather Understand

Given senior management's primary role and obligation to manage the business properly, IROs are tasked with marketing the company's stock with investors and fielding the far majority of questions. It is important to keep in mind that these marketing efforts are not merely to best position your company, nor are they to convince potential shareholders to buy the stock or to encourage existing shareholders to buy more. Rather, while the company has a fiduciary responsibility to create and protect shareholder value, the most effective IR marketing efforts enable the investment community to simply *understand the company,* including its strategy, operational results, financial expectations, and market position vis-à-vis its competition.

By effectively communicating with the investment community and by offering an appropriate level of access to management, true understanding can occur. Accordingly, investors will make a fair and informed investment decision even if they decide to merely hold the company's stock or even sell it at this point in time. By fostering this type of open dialogue and credibility with Wall Street, and by being simply accessible and candid in both good times and bad, investors will likely revisit the stock seriously if and when the company's operational story becomes more attractive.

The Custom Tailored Suit, The "Heart of The Art"

Tailoring the company's messages to the appropriate level of investor and analyst interest is a central theme underlying the art of truly effective communication. In my opinion, Cisco's legendary CEO John Chambers uniquely understands and masters this principle, ranking him among the most effective CEOs in technology management. Understanding the value of moderating corporate messages holds true for the practice of Investor Relations, as the level of investor interest should dictate the level of detail provided during your limited time together.

While some investors and analysts may desire detailed information on every contract nuance and balance sheet detail, others remain quite pleased with high-level overviews and broader philosophical discussions. As an example, in many cases European analysts and investors tend to focus on the big picture, while many U.S. investors and analysts can be extremely focused on quarterly earnings results and expectations. The result of this difference in bias is that U.S. analysts may react more to an earnings miss of $0.01 per share while European analysts may place less emphasis on this metric and focus on other aspects of the results. I am in no way knocking U.S. analysts or their investment rationales. On the contrary, I have enjoyed working with some of them and believe that they are perhaps the most detail-oriented analysts in the world. Regardless, understanding the values of each investor and analyst will be insightful and useful to you as an IRO. Likewise, quickly assessing the level of background knowledge on the company and its industry should guide the IRO's level of discussion into a most useful one for the client.

Considering the IRO as a partner to the investment community is a helpful psychology as investors and analysts seek to develop understanding, albeit with the inherent boundaries that exist with respect to proprietary information, ethics and legal considerations.

Develop An Annual IR Plan, And Execute Against It Consistency

While the nature of Investor Relations is often reactive to developments of competitors, industry merger and acquisition activity, new product introductions, customer contracts, market share reports and press releases, it is essential that marketing efforts to the financial community include diligent annual planning and goal setting.

The annual IR plan is an opportunity for the IRO to highlight the accomplishments of the previous year, to analyze the past year and to modify and reprioritize for the year ahead. The tendency for an IR effort to be largely reactive to market developments and requests and less proactive is a very real concern. In my opinion, the time and effort used to develop an annual IR plan for the year ahead is highly valuable and necessary. Consistently setting and executing against your own agenda will prove valuable to the overall IR effort.

Based on the finite financial and operational resources at hand, a clear and well thought out Investor Relations plan will outline all key elements of the company's anticipated institutional meetings program and retail shareholder events. While the annual IR plan must be distributed to and "blessed" by senior management, it must be executed by a capable team; often one with diverse backgrounds and skills.

Delivering a best in class investor program must be based on a clear and thorough planning process based on continual iteration, feedback and adjustment. Highly interactive weekly or bi-weekly "meetings meetings" are often necessary to keep a detailed program on track. At these meetings, all upcoming and requested IR activities are reviewed - often looking out as far as eighteen months. A "hyperactive" IR program within a large corporation is itself a ship that needs to be steered by a capable, if not somewhat paranoid, IRO.

When formulating the annual IR plan it is essential that management recognize that Wall Street values consistency above all other factors - consistent earnings, consistent views on the market and even consistent management appearances at industry events such as conferences and trade shows. As a result, it is important that consistency be not just an IR goal, but also be a philosophy that its senior management embraces. Long-term shareholder value can only be created by continuous and consistent performance and IR programs that also have these characteristics will be best understood and embraced by the financial community.

Drive Hyperactive Investor Relations Programs

While it is up to each company's senior management team to decide how large the IR program is to be in terms of its financial budget and human resources, the IRO must drive its Investor Relations program with the available resources at hand. Senior management will generally be highly receptive to proposed changes and modifications to the existing IR effort if they improve the quality of the program.

The more active an IR program is, the more likely investors will be to truly understand the company and make an informed investment opinion about whether or not they want to buy more of the company's stock, hold what the have, or sell it. While effectively communicating with investors and analysts is the primary goal of Investor Relations efforts, those members of the investment community that decide to sell the stock in the near term or place a Hold or Sell recommendation on the stock may be more likely to purchase or recommend the stock in the future when fundamentals improve if simply given a continual flow information as incremental progress is made.

An effective IR effort involves many tactical aspects, but high up on the list of priorities is to continually reinforce the company's ever-changing circumstances and strategy to the investment community. The IR team must communicate the company's position on various industry issues in a timely and extremely responsive manner, and design and implement creative vehicles for extensive investor and analyst interaction with management at many levels.

Investor Relations Team, Don't Over Protect Your Management

While the IR team is tasked with the daily responsibility for the company's investors, they are clearly regarded internally as management's front line with respect to handling most inquiries. External constituents likewise acknowledge that most day-to-day clarifications and corporate updates are not to be provided by members of either senior or operational management. However, while IR is the front line with respect to most inquiries and should field the majority of investor and analyst inquiries, it is critical that IROs avoid over sheltering their management team and give the investment community the periodic access that they need.

By over-sheltering management, IROs risk isolating the very investors and analysts they are tasked with serving, often unbeknownst to management. Analysts that feel that they are being treated with less importance then they deserve are likely to swiftly turn their attention to those companies that offer them better management access – where they receive first hand feedback from management on the complex issues at hand. In my view, it is easier for analysts to write insightful research on a company that is open with its management time. While the number of interactions that the investment community has with members of senior management should be managed to maximize the use of executive time, analyst and investor interactions with senior management should never be entirely eliminated by the IRO.

While analysts and investors should receive a fair amount of tine directly with members of management, there are often times when members of the investment community may actually prefer a meeting with an IRO rather than a senior executive. This is often the case if the analyst is not fully "up to speed" on a particular issue.

If an analyst follows the company closely, being proactive in offering management time is very much appreciated by the investment community. If perhaps for nothing more than sheer satisfaction, it is desirable to offer access, proactively. IROs that proactively seek to establish meetings and conference calls with senior members of management, will earn undying gratitude from the analyst they support.

Analysts May Prefer Meeting With Investor Relations

While a meeting with a company's well trained IRO might not seem nearly as valued as meeting with the company's senior management, many portfolio managers and analysts often have a greater comfort level with meeting with the IRO. With analysts traveling nearly constantly, they may feel simply unprepared and uncomfortable talking to the company's CEO or CFO. Analysts may feel that they are not "up to speed" on the latest issues or financial guidance, and fear asking questions that are well known to those following the stock closer. A more informal update from a trusted member of the Investor Relations team might be preferred instead. Over the course of a year, it would not be uncommon for members of the investment community to have a hundred hours of one-on-one interaction with a company's IRO, if not more. Simply being comfortable with the level of discussion taking place is a key element to analyst satisfaction.

Strategic and Budgetary Considerations

Each corporate management team makes strategic decisions about the size of the IR team and the budgetary resources allocated to the function itself. As it does so, Wall Street is attune to these actions and may make assumptions as to its relative importance to the company. A well-staffed and well-informed IR team that is very accessible to analysts and investors alike, may be view as having its act together. Accordingly, the investment community may extrapolate that other areas of the business are given as much attention. For if the company approaches its customers in the same thoughtful manner as it does its investors, it is likely that its customers will tend to be satisfied and loyal.

On the other hand, if it is difficult to reach a member of the IR team to ask questions, clarify the company's position on a particular or urgent topic, the company might not be sending the right signals to its investors. Certainly, if investors infer that it is as difficult for the company's customers to reach a knowledgeable salesperson as it is for an investor or analyst to reach an informative IR contact, they may infer that the company isn't managed very well. Accordingly, it is important for management to adequately invest in the IR function given that its staff is often very small in relation to the company's total employee base, but are highly influential in the minds of investors and their decisions.

The question of how large of a group is necessary to function well depends on the management team and the quality of the people in the group. In some companies, including many medium sized ones, the IR function is handled almost exclusively by the company's Treasurer or CFO. In other companies, a team of up to twenty highly specialized individuals market the company on a daily basis. While we view the latter case as excessive, a group of seven to ten is more than adequate for most Fortune 500 companies. In our view, the team can begin to hit its stride with about four to six members and can refine its task set very nicely with additional resources. As an IR effort expands with additional staffers, care must be taken to carefully manage the group, their expanding efforts and each members' more limited scope of responsibility.

2

Understanding The Buy-side

When an Investor Relations effort sets out to market the company's stock to the institutional investment community it has to balance its limited resources with the needs of both the so-called "buy-side" and "sell-side" segments of the institutional investment community. The "buy-side" is composed of both buy-side portfolio managers and the analyst that covers the sector at each money management firm. Due to the fact that the buy-side is responsible for managing significant amounts of money directly, they represent an influential constituency. That said, they do not generally publish research externally and often keep their opinions on companies within their respective firms. Their research and opinions are generally proprietary and used for internal decision making purposes.

Given that buy-side research is generally not published externally, it is often difficult for an IRO to know exactly what price target, rating or even what opinion a buy-side analyst has on the stock. In those instances, the quarterly reports that money managers are required to file with the SEC, outlining their position in specific securities, can be monitored closely by a stock surveillance firm to detect net changes in shares held. Monitoring these changes may offer insight into the buy-side analyst's rating and decisions made by its portfolio managers. However, even while a particular buy-side analyst may be strongly opposed to ownership in the company you represent, the firm's portfolio managers may indeed buy and hold positions in the stock and go against the recommendation of the firm's analyst. Conversely, while a buy-side analyst may strongly favor a particular stock and rate the company quite highly, one of the firm's portfolio managers may opt instead not to purchase the stock as recommended by its analyst on a belief that the company is already fairly valued and priced for perfection in execution.

Additionally, the buy-side firm may have various investment funds with different investment objectives, such as investing primarily in so-called value and income stocks. While we will discuss these in more detail, the portfolio manager of a value fund may not invest in a particular stock by virtue of a stock's price to earnings ratio being in excess of 10, while the manager of an income fund may rule the same stock out by virtue of its dividend yield being below 4%. However, the manager of an aggressive growth fund may overweight its position in the stock, as recommended by the analyst, with less concern over P/E ratios and dividend yields, in favor of expanding market opportunities and the likelihood of expanding earnings and earnings multiples over time. Such a portfolio manager may be willing to pay more for such a stock, as it may suit his fund's profile better than that of a more conservative value or income fund.

In instances where the portfolio manager goes against the rating of its analyst, he or she may be following a gut feeling about the stock or may be following the recommendations of external "sell-side" analysts, which also provide the firm with research. Sell-side analysts generally market their research to buy-side portfolio managers and internal buy-side sector analysts alike. Given that both buy-side analysts and portfolio managers typically cover a large number of stocks, they often, but not always, rely on the sell side for detailed financial models and research. I have known some outstanding analysts on the buy-side, whose insights were quite impressive. Every money management firm is different in their reliance on external and internal research.

Various Fund Investment Objectives, From Capital Preservation to Aggressive Growth

The term "buy side" refers to all institutional money management firms, regardless of their investment objectives. These firms can manage the assets of individual investors, corporations, public and private pension funds, and even sub-manage assets from *other* buy-side money management firms. With many different types of investors, specific fund investment objectives can differ greatly from those seeking primarily investments that provide capital preservation with a stable dividend payout (income stocks or bonds) to those seeking aggressive share price appreciation (growth stocks). Risky stocks that target aggressive growth are often called momentum stocks.

In the case of funds which seek capital preservation and income, portfolio managers running these funds will typically seek an array of income-producing investments such as utility companies with high dividend yields and a long history of stable revenue streams and good profitability. In the case of managers focused on share price appreciation and growth, portfolio managers are more likely to consider technology investments, although they often carry significantly higher valuations, risk profiles and appreciation potential.

Just as diversification across many industry sectors limits risk, so too does geographic diversification. For those individuals inclined to invest outside the United States, there are an assortment of non-U.S. investment funds available as well.

Typical Fund Restrictions

Many firms prohibit investing in companies whose share prices are below a certain threshold (often $5 per share) or have market capitalizations below a certain value. Funds are also generally prohibited from purchasing more that a certain percentage of a company's outstanding shares. In these ways, funds are restricted from ownership in equities that are expected to be highly volatile or relatively illiquid investments.

While mutual funds have specific restrictions and goals, investing in any investment vehicle requires ongoing monitoring of the fund's performance. It is not uncommon for portfolio managers to have medium or short tenures at the helm of a particular fund, given the relative success or failure of their efforts at exceeding or underperforming relative to their benchmark indexes. As such, the human talent behind a fund can change quickly. So too can a fund's name. At one time, Fidelity's Aggressive Growth Fund was once called the Emerging Growth Fund. While the fund's name seemingly implied a focus toward investing in smaller companies, a significant percentage of the fund's assets were invested in larger technology companies. While the fund was not restricted from investing in larger companies, the name of the fund was changed to better reflect its portfolio's composition. It is wise for individual investors to monitor and adjust allocations for all investments, including investments in actively managed mutual funds as well as investments in individual stocks.

Fund Research and Investing Orientation

Many of the larger institutions employ their own industry sector analysts to aid portfolio managers in their investment decisions, making recommendations and providing internal, proprietary research and analysis. Smaller institutions may not have this luxury and tend to rely to a greater extent on sell-side analysts to provide the majority of their research and analysis needs. While many smaller firms do not have industry sector analysts, they tend to have more broadly-focused analysts, known as "generalists." Generally speaking, buy-side analysts tend to cover a notably larger number of companies than their sell-side counterparts.

Institutional investment firms charge an annual management fee based on the percentage of assets under management; which generally ranges from 1% to 2%.

Most "index funds," those funds that attempt to simply mirror the performance of the major stock market indexes, such as the S&P500, are generally lower than more actively managed funds given that they invest only in the companies that make up the index, and often at a proportional level to their weighting in the index. Given that they are mirroring the performance of the benchmark index, little fundamental research on individual stocks is conducted and their management fees are generally low. Index funds are vehicles for individual investors to invest in a diversified basket of stocks, generally with low minimum investments. On the other hand, most actively managed mutual funds charge management fees that can vary greatly, but do not generally top 2% of assets under management as a general rule. Similar to index funds, most actively managed mutual funds generally have low minimum investments as well, on the order of $500.

Hedge Funds

Investing in hedge funds is not generally a vehicle that is available to most individual investors, given that they often have large minimum investments. Hedge funds often have a limited number of investors of high net worth. Often structured as private partnerships, minimum investments are typically on the order of $1 million.

Hedge fund managers are generally compensated by a percentage of any profits earned by the fund. This additional profit sharing fee is typically 20% and is clearly an inventive for hedge fund managers to perform well. The variety of hedge funds and hedge fund investment strategies is extremely varied. While hedge funds can take 'long' positions, those holdings that are expected to go higher, they can also 'short' positions, those that are expected to go lower. As such, hedge funds can theoretically make money when securities go higher or lower. Among their investment alternatives, they can invest in stocks, high-yield bonds, arbitrage convertible bonds, trade currencies and employ highly sophisticated modeling and risk management techniques. Hedge fund managers often purchase warrants and options (puts and calls) to help capitalize and leverage their potential investment returns and borrow leverage their potential returns by borrowing money. Many firms are considered "global macro" in nature and focus their attention on global trends and currency trading, some of which is done with highly quantitative and proprietary "black box" analyses.

As their name implies, they also seek to hedge their risk by having *both* long and short positions at the same time.

Traditional index funds and mutual funds generally do no have the ability to short stocks and utilize options and other such complex investment tools and strategies. Therefore most index funds and mutual funds will only appreciate in value when stocks rise, in bull markets.

Hedge funds on the other hand can earn profits when stocks advance during bull markets, if they are net long on the right investments, but can also earn profit when stocks decline in bear markets, if they are net short on the right investments. As of early 2006, global hedge fund assets are approximately $1 trillion, a small sum relative to the amount invested in mutual funds. With the interest in hedge funds increasing rapidly, hedge fund assets under management should grow notable higher. Given the significant performance incentive, many of the best minds in the asset management industry are joining, or starting their own, hedge funds.

The Evolution of Investment Alternatives:
From Individual Stocks and Bonds To Mutual Funds

Exchange traded funds (ETFs) and hedge funds are perhaps the most significant new investment vehicle introduced for retail investors over the past few years. First lets briefly talk about the selection process of individual stocks, actively managed mutual funds and passive index funds.

Individual Stock and Bond Selection

Given that buying an individual stock is generally based on a belief that it will outperform other investment alternatives, an investor must perform significant due diligence on the company of interest, its broader industry and its competition. Many investors also purchase a variety of bonds to generate income and reduce volatility of the broader portfolio. Bond alternatives include corporate bonds, municipal bonds and U.S. Treasury obligations. Of course, investments in bonds also carry investment risk and should be considered carefully.

After purchasing a diversified basket of individual stocks and bonds, ongoing monitoring of the investments is equally as important. As such, the investor must provide ongoing management of his or her own portfolio but may or may not have adequate time to appropriately dedicate to the task. To address this need, mutual funds assembled pools of investor capital and professionally selected and managed stocks and bonds, reducing the risk associated with making larger investments in fewer specific securities. While the construction of a diverse equity or bond portfolios helps reduce security-specific risk, such a portfolio would remain subject to a degree of market risk.

Mutual Fund Selection

Often with limited time to devote to actively managing a diverse investment portfolio, individual investors are able to choose from a massive array of mutual funds. In selecting a mutual fund, investors need to thoroughly research such items as historical performance and portfolio composition; review the background of the fund's portfolio manager; study various management fees (front-end or back-end "loads" or fees); and be careful to match their own objectives with those of their mutual fund selections.

To diversify their risk profile associated with any one mutual fund selection, investors often divide their investments between multiple mutual funds, such as those targeting growth or income. Additionally, many investors have a balance of funds that focus on small, mid and large-capitalization stocks. Others further diversify by geography, such as funds that focus on investments in emerging markets. Some focus on an extraordinarily level of investment granularity and invest exclusively on the securities of such niche markets as telecommunications equipment or semiconductors. Mutual funds also focus on many investment niches, including those that focus on environmentally friendly or "green" companies. As with individual stocks, investors must spend ample time reviewing and monitoring investments in mutual funds.

The portfolio manager of a mutual fund determines the desired amount of each stock in the fund. As such, mutual funds are generally actively managed in nature. Individual investors can redeem the value of their holdings at Net Asset Value (NAV). Given that mutual funds are not traded intra-day, as are individual stocks, mutual fund redemptions are generally made after the close of the financial markets and after the calculation of the mutual fund's daily NAV calculation. Mutual funds still remain the investment vehicle of choice for retirement accounts, such as 401Ks.

Index Mutual Funds

Index funds are mutual funds that invest in the securities that make up a particular index, such as the Standard & Poors 500, Nasdaq 100 or Dow Jones Industrials 50. Index mutual funds are far less actively managed. Rather, index funds are monitored and adjusted to ensure that the composition of the fund mirrors the composition and weighting of each stock in the index whose performance it is being emulated. As a result, the management fee for investing in index funds is often significantly lower than the management fee associated with more actively managed mutual funds that require more research and trading. Index mutual funds are also redeemed upon calculation of NAV after market close, as are all mutual funds.

The Evolution of Investment Alternatives:
From Exchange Traded Funds (ETFs) and Hedge Funds

Exchange Traded Funds

Exchange Traded Funds (EFTs) allow investors to directly purchase those stocks that make up an index, such as the S&P 500, Nasdaq 100 or Dow Jones Industrials 50, in direct proportion to their composition or weighting in the index. Rather than have management oversight similar to that of a traditional mutual fund and pay ongoing management fees, the investor simply purchases the appropriate ETF on the open market.

As an example, in order to purchase the ETF of the S&P 500 or the Nasdaq 100, the investor would simply purchase ticker symbols SPY or QQQQ, respectively. ETFs are traded in real time, during market hours rather than upon the market close at Net Asset Value. At present, while there are not nearly as many ETFs as there are mutual funds, purchasing them is an easy and uncomplicated way for investors to invest in the broader markets. Among others, Barclays I-shares is a large provider of ETFs. The management fees associated with ETF investments are low relative to many actively managed and index mutual funds.

Hedge Funds

While we have already discussed hedge funds in detail, clearly hedge funds are attracting the attention and capital of high net worth investors. It is important to note that liquidity is generally lower with hedge funds than many investment alternatives. Among the most illiquid investments are hedge funds, private equity funds and real estate investments. Liquidity should be a consideration to any investment. And while the number of hedge funds has increased rapidly over the past few years, and returns have been difficult for many managers, in my view hedge funds assets will continue to grow. In my view, high net worth individual investors are increasingly considering hedge fund assets as a new asset class. As a result, the asset class offers the benefit of diversification.

3

The Retail Investment Community

Retail investors include all segments of individual investors, including retirees, individuals saving for retirement, parents saving for their children's college educations and those saving for a rainy day. Accordingly, most individual investors seek a range of income, capital appreciation and growth. Some have a tolerance for risk and fluctuation of the value of their investments while other have very little.

Often individual investors buy stocks and hold them for the long-term, awaiting capital appreciation and collecting periodic dividend payments along the way. Hence, many investors are said to be 'long' in their positions, making the call that the stocks in their portfolio will tend to appreciate. While some retail investors follow the developments in the holdings on a minute-by-minute basis, as do most institutional money managers, many others monitor their investments on a more infrequent basis.

While a generality, many individual investors tend to buy companies with solid brand names, often household names such as Coke, General Electric and Citigroup. They often seek more stable investments with good earnings and dividend payment histories.

Certainly, there are individual investors with much larger tolerance for risk, and are more attracted to aggressive investments rather than conservative ones. Among individual investors, one segment in particular - The Day Trader – often assumes an extremely high degree of risk, trading in and out of long and short positions in an effort to capture short-term profits. While some Day Traders look upon their efforts as a part-time effort, others trade stocks full-time, seeking to make their living from the practice.

Day Trading

Day Traders are particularly interesting to study because they are unlike most other individual investors. Not only are these individuals often fairly eccentric, they often utilize highly sophisticated quantitative research tools and basic charting techniques such as moving averages and trend lines. Broadband access to the Internet, low cost electronic trading platforms such Ameritrade and the vast amounts of corporate and market data from countless sources, including FirstCall, Bloomberg, Dow Jones, Reuters and PR Newswire are readily available. Day traders often utilize significant quantitative analytical tools and understand macro demand trends quite well, although they often spend less time understanding the complex operational issues facing a company such specific product life cycles, corporate strategies, and new product developments issues. Individual analysts and money managers often focus more on these latter elements than day traders.

Day trading one's own personal capital can be quite a risky experience and many day traders often attempt to capitalize on individual stock price declines as well as broader market declines by 'shorting' stocks the way institutional hedge fund managers do. However, institutional traders generally have various proprietary research tools available to help them manage their general exposure and risk profiles. Many day traders and institutional hedge funds often purchase warrants and options (puts and calls) to help capitalize and leverage their potential investment returns.

Clearly, technology has evolved to support trading at home and Internet-based applications such as access to real-time news wire services. Individuals have notable access to corporate press releases and web pages, company profiles, investor conference calls and detailed SEC filings. They also have access to the on-line versions of various print newspapers such as the Wall Street Journal and New York Times, and network programming, CNN, CNBC and CBS Marketwatch. Individual investors have access to vast amounts of information. Along with excellent access to real-time and historical information, individual investors today have many trading tools available such as real-time trading programs offered by Ameritrade and Fidelity. In many respects, the Internet forever changed investing the way it changed communication and commerce.

However, large institutional investors generally have even more advanced tools and proprietary equity research available to them. These institutions spend significant amounts of money to develop and maintain state-of-the-art information systems and trading capabilities, proprietary trading algorithms, programmed trading tools. But beyond basic technology-based tools, institutional analysts and portfolio managers often have a significant amount of additional information available to them including a vast network of contacts in the industry; access directly to other financial analysts and portfolio managers; access to company management teams, consultants, and market research firms; proprietary internal company and sector research reports and financial models; and numerous contacts within companies themselves. Clearly, large institutions have additional capital resources available to them, which can create a better feel for the market and the 'buzz' around a specific stock. Hence, day trading can be a very risky profession, or hobby, indeed. To some extent in my view, the euphoria of the late 1990s stock bubble was in part fueled by unprecedented investor access to advanced capital markets trading tools.

Retail Stocks

Securities with strong retail orientation, such as McDonalds would naturally have a fairly high percentage of its stock held by individuals who are familiar with the company's strong brand and retail strength are attracted to the company's long-history of revenue and earnings growth. While the company's stock has had challenging periods due to various reasons, including a trend in more healthy fare and the introduction of its ultra-low priced menu items, the company remains viewed by some as a "cult stock," similar to the following that many still hold for the likes of GE, Cisco Systems and Apple Computer. With a loyal core investor following, cult stocks inherently trade at a premium. Operational and management excellence drives investor attention toward certain companies and investors expect nothing less than excellent execution, in everything that the company does – including Investor Relations.

Conservative Equity Investors

Conservative investors, both retail and institutional, often invest in equities that have long-established dividend payment histories, such as public utilities. Public utilities often trade in a similar fashion to bonds, tending to increase in value when momentum and aggressive growth-oriented equities decline and decrease in value when such equities rise. Many investors, including the venerable Warren Buffet, have avoided technology stocks like the plague. They have done so for countless years, even while the bull market of the mid-1990s led to great criticism of their conservative investing styles and the underperforming nature of their equity portfolios. The investment community was reminded of the benefits of conservative investing and conservative genius when the basic brick and mortar investments they held continued to perform relatively well after the Internet and tech bubbles ended. Many investors fled the volatile equities markets and embraced fixed income investments and real estate. For many investors today, a conservative investment style is the only one they will make after watching their 401K and brokerage statements deteriorate during the euphoria of the late 1990s.

4

Understanding The Sell-side

Sell-side analysts and their brokerage firms aggressively market their research products to buy-side analysts and portfolio managers. In many regards, the buy-side is inundated with sell-side research reports, e-mail newsletters, voice mail updates, conferences and requests for meetings and trading authorizations and analyst votes. Among the key differences between the sell-side and the buy-side is that members of the sell-side are generally not involved with managing money directly and hence with purchasing individual stocks. Sell-side analysts typically focus on an a relatively small number of stocks, conducting and writing research on their every development. They are often relied upon by the buy-side to generate financial forecasting models and insightful research on their industry sector and companies under their coverage. It can be generalized that the group essentially sells its research to members of the buy-side. Additionally, while not always the case, sell-side firms are often involved in investment banking initiatives to corporations. At these firms, investment bankers often help their corporate clients engage in initial public offers (IPOs), secondary offerings, and various other strategic advisory roles.

The prominence of the sector analyst at the sell-side firm can be an influential factor in a corporation's decision to select the investment banking services of a broker-dealer. The role of investment banking in relation to research opinions has been a topic of conversation for some time, as some investors believe that if a sell-side firm has investment banking business with a particular corporation, that its research opinions may be compromised. While a so-called "Chinese Wall" is said to exist between the research and investment banking departments of a brokerage firm, some investors believe that the opinions of analysts with such ties should be taken with a grain of salt, believing that a firm's existing investment banking relationships may be a factor in the firm's rating on the stock. Additionally, in the absence of an investment banking relationship, some investors may be skeptical on the firm's stock ratings or opinions given that the broker dealer may indeed be courting an investment banking relationship with the company and that it might issue bullish research in support of such efforts.

Disclosure rules require broker-dealers to disclose any investment banking ties clearly on research reports and also require analysts to disclose whether or not they hold securities of firms under their coverage. Regardless, some sell-side firms such as Bernstein Research, Argus Research and Fulcrum Global Partners do not provide corporate investment banking services whatsoever, believing that their inherently unbiased research earns them credibility in the eyes of the investor clients. Brokerage firms with both research and investment banking divisions have further separated their investment banking and research divisions to clear up any controversy.

While the sell-side analyst is responsible for generating timely, insightful, and objective research, each sell-side firm has a sales force that promotes this research to buy-side portfolio managers and sector analysts. The sell-side markets their ideas to members of the buy-side by publishing research in various forms, including distribution via the First Call newswire, e-mail, voice-mail, and by conducting in-person visits. While on the road meeting with institutions, an analyst is generally accompanied by an institutional salesperson, which is responsible for maintaining the overall relationship with the buy-side firm and for securing commission revenues. Trading would is done by the brokerage firm's traders, who in turn have trading counterparts on the buy-side.

The buy-side generally looks to the sell-side as idea generators and suppliers of information as they seek to make wise investment selections. Within a typical industry sector, the sell-side analyst community may consist of as many as forty or even fifty analysts covering the sector. Some of the analysts at these brokerage firms are more likely to be conservative and "go with the flow" of industry opinion, while others are more likely to be aggressive and make bold calls about particular stocks or the overall industry. It is not uncommon for some sell-side analysts to make bold sector calls, downgrading or upgrading many if not all the stocks in their coverage universe at the same time. Rating changes typically attracts attention from the buy-side and the press and can sometimes make or break an analyst's career. Some sell-side firms themselves seem more prone to this type of activity and a skeptic would say that their actions are geared toward making noise in an effort to drive trading revenues by encouraging buy-side clients to buy or sell stocks. Above all, the buy-side desires and values high-quality, objective and insightful research. Many investment managers use independent analysts and research to ensure that their research is free of potential conflicts of interest.

Sell-side Revenue Sources

Sell-side analysts and their brokerage firms compete with each other for limited trading commissions from institutions. Sell-side commissions are generated associated with the level of buy-side trading activity with approximately two to five cents of commission going to the sell-side firm for every share that the buy-side firm decides to trade with a particular sell-side firm. If a sell-side analyst generates insightful ideas that ultimately help a portfolio manager or buy-side analyst make good calls on stocks, helping the institution make money in the market, they are likely to reward the sell-side brokerage firm with trading commission revenues and analyst votes. Analyst votes usually translate into trading commissions, which in turn represent a primary source of revenues for the sell-side brokerage firm.

Another revenue source for the sell-side is its corporate investment banking initiatives. Brokerage firms with investment banking divisions hope to generate investment banking revenues from corporations by creating strategic advisory relationships, creating primary or secondary public offerings, issuing debt and generating various fees associated with finding and negotiating mergers and acquisitions. Minimum investment banking fees are generally in the range of $1 million, although smaller firms often have a lower threshold.

Often the sell-side also has:

- Internal traders managing some of the firm's capital;

- Prime brokerage operations where the firm execute trades for its hedge fund client base, and also extends leverage to them;

- Hedge funds where it manages others' capital; and

- Traditional mutual fund operations.

A good example of the diversification of business lines are the current structures of J.P. Morgan, Morgan Stanley, Goldman Sachs.

"Institutional Investor" Rankings

While sell-side analysts compete for votes from institutional portfolio managers and analysts, they are also rated by a few independent organizations, such as Institutional Investor (I.I.) magazine and The Wall Street Journal. By far, the most influential sell-side ranking comes from I.I., which surveys buy-side institutions for their views on the best analysts in each market sector. Most sell-side brokerage firms have moderate pressure for analysts to be recognized in I.I. rankings, and attainment of I.I. rankings 1, 2, or 3 are highly complimentary of the firm's analyst. In certain market sectors however, with as many as 40 to 50 sell side brokerage firms vying for institutional trading activity, being at the top of the I.I. rankings remains illusive for many sector analysts.

Institutional and Retail Shareholders

As each corporation has a mix of both institutional shareholders and retail shareholders alike, each of these vastly different sets of constituents requires vastly different marketing and communications efforts. While these two categories represent the IRO's primary external constituents, within each there are many subcategories that warrant special attention and insight. In developing an effective and comprehensive Investor Relations plan, it is essential that management analyze its retail and institutional shareholder base very closely to determine the appropriate level of resources allocated to each.

The percentage of retail and institutional shareholders that hold the company's equity depends greatly on factors such as whether the company's products are highly technical in nature or primarily derived from the retail market, the strength of its brand, size of its advertising budget, its dividend payment history, and even whether the financial markets are enjoying a bull market or suffering from a bear market.

In order to attract more stable retail shareholders (volatile day traders aside), the company can increase its quarterly dividend, making the company's dividend annual yield more attractive to individuals and mutual funds that seek high dividend yields. While the IR team can easily track the percentage of retail and institutional ownership and monitor the effects of such dividend adjustments, existing IR resources can also be redirected, while new resources can be added to support additional program elements if deemed necessary. In this case, management may decide to further expand or initiate a dedicated retail shareholder marketing effort.

The overall Investor Relations strategy should include various programs to market a company's stock to the institutional investment community, both the buy-side and the sell-side, as well as directly to retail investors.

5

Dynamic Investor Relations Programs

IR Programs For *All* Investor Categories

An effective Investor Relations strategy must include various programs to market a company's stock to various members of the financial community, which includes both the institutional investment community (both the buy-side and the sell-side), as well as the individual (or retail) community. The needs of these two constituents differ greatly and so to will the programs used by the Investor Relations team to effectively market the company's stock. As an IRO, many retail shareholders and institutions will be a very good or natural fit with the profile of your company's industry, market position, dividend payment history or even growth history.

An effective strategy focuses on identifying your existing shareholder base, targeting those that are critical and further targeting other firms that you believe have either no position in your company or have under-invested in it or your sector. There are various approaches used to create an Investor Relations program that executes on the various opportunities at hand. These approaches include coordinating individual one-on-one meetings, group-meetings, topic-specific conference calls and quarterly earnings-based conference calls. We will discuss the merits of each of these to a greater extent in subsequent chapters.

As with all effective programs, coordinating the details of these efforts are critical. Every Investor Relations activity has a degree of risk associated with it. With all meetings and disclosures to the financial community are on the public record, regardless of how casual or formal the setting may appear. Both the Investor Relations officer and management are highly public figures and you are fully representing the company. As such, each interaction with various members of the financial community should be considered public, on the record, and reflect such sensitivity.

The selection of corporate spokespersons to the financial community is a critical element of an effective program. Selecting someone with a limited industry or technical background may not have adequate credibility to represent a technical company, while one without good communication skills or financial skills can prove equally harmful to the company's image. Institutional investors can invest in any company that they chose, and can dismiss one if they are not provided an adequate level of information or do not believe they are getting proper attention.

Other strategic decisions on the part of the Investor Relations officer include selecting the timing and frequency of communications to the investment community, as well as deciding and reviewing their content and level of complexity. As we explore the details of an effective program, it will become clear that managing an effective Investor Relations program is an art as opposed to a science, although structuring an effective IR program requires thorough planning and disciplined processes.

The Dynamic Investor Relations Program, Modify Your Target Audience

Portfolio managers of value-based mutual funds are generally unwilling to pay a significant premium for stocks. In the mid to late 1990s, many portfolio managers of value stocks, such as those at Boston-based Eaton Vance, were skeptical about the rise in value of technology stocks such as Nortel Networks. As a result, value investors and value-oriented mutual funds remained largely on the sidelines in relation to telecom stocks. However, as the telecom market came under significant contraction, value-based investors generally became interested in monitoring the developments of the technology sector, as the entire sector came under pressure.

When stocks such as Lucent and Nortel dipped toward 50 cents per share in 2002, watchful value investors purchased them, while traditional investors in technology stocks, growth and momentum investors, saw little earnings growth on the horizon. As these value investors saw their newly acquired shares rise to above $2 per share, stock in these companies still traded at approximately 1x annual revenues and the stocks were fairly valued based on many analysts' financial assumptions and forecasts. The rise in share price happened relatively fast, and represented a significant amount of capital appreciation for those investors that saw value at such price levels.

Naturally, IR marketing efforts to value investors would have been quite difficult in the telecom heyday, as the Price-Earnings and Price-Earnings-Growth ratios that were placed on tech stocks by growth and aggressive growth investors made them too expensive for value investors to generally purchase. But when as the market changed, so too did the need for an effective investors relations program to market the company's stock less with institutional money managers that had aggressive growth and core growth biases and more toward those with "growth at a reasonable price" (GARP) and value orientations. As revenue and earnings growth once again returns to an industry, marketing efforts by companies in that industry should naturally shift toward those with growth biases. IR programs need to be fluid with respect to their institutional targeting activities.

During the high-flying days of the mid- to late-1990s, investors in many technology companies were composed largely of institutional investors, such as growth-oriented mutual funds and hedge funds. These institutions focused heavily on capturing growth and anticipated significant capital appreciation of technology shares. These technology stocks generally paid very little, if any, quarterly dividends and these investors were generally not concerned with dividend payments. Rather, they anticipated significant growth in revenue and earnings, which they believed would further appreciate the price of the underlying equity security.

On the other hand, many utility stocks are historically very consistent in paying income in the form of quarterly dividends. Income-yielding equities are often purchased by individual investors that are generally conservative in nature and are principally concerned with the preservation of capital, as opposed to capital appreciation. Intuitively, investing in technology shares is more risky than investing in income-oriented stocks. But during the mid- and late-1990s, investing in technology shares was a fairly solid way to capitalize on the reward associated with such risky investments.

We know all too well that when the rally ended, the element of risk became clearer than ever, which for some time was less evident during the long-running bull market. And within the general categories of institutional and retail, there exist great disparities in terms of risk tolerance. Retirees that were most comfortable investing in CDs and bonds throughout the 1990s were later joined by many investors seeking safe havens for their assets after the financial markets faltered.

For an IRO, there is a natural tendency to focus the far majority of time on those investors which best fit your current investment profile, as those individuals will naturally be most receptive to your story. However, it is important to spend time and attention on those that do not meet your profile, and may have long remained on the sidelines. Over time they too may become more interested in your company as both your company, its broader industry and the markets evolve to more attractive levels.

Excellent Execution and Processes Drive Investor Attention, And Possibly Corporate Market Valuations

When customers, competitors, investors and others benchmark the corporate practices of best-in-class companies, inevitably many are struck with envy and wonder as to why other companies don't have such disciplined processes. We cite the highly disciplined book-close process of Cisco Systems, and the sheer brand and marketing genius of Disney and McDonalds.

As one example, Cisco can close its books in a mere 24 hours and perform a virtual book close at any time in the quarter. Excellence with programs of this nature enable investors to gain a level of comfort with their investments, by trusting that their investment remains in capable management hands. Investors may believe that when Cisco's CEO speaks publicly, he is very likely aware of the quarter-to-date financials. Cisco's financial processes and systems are capable of reviewing results by operating unit, product and even by individual salesperson.

By employing the Internet to enable employees to individually select benefits (i.e., "employee self service") and train employees with video clips distributed globally over Web servers, Cisco saves millions of dollars of human resources expenses that many other companies bear. Investors, quite simply, are often willing to pay a premium for companies that can manage their business this well.

Disciplined processes pay dividends handsomely in the minds of investors and it is critical for corporate management to drive numerous such processes throughout the company, including but not limited to your investor program. Accordingly, investor interest in your company and its equity and debt obligations may rise notably.

6

Investor Relations Team Structure

There are two primary ways that most IR programs allocate their line resources. The first approach, which we generally prefer, is for the firm's resources to be categorized into two segments: those individuals serving the institutional community and those serving the retail community. Another approach is to organize the team by their interaction with the sell-side and buy-side. In this way, members of your team will be organized to focus on programs for either publishing sell-side analysts or buy-side institutional money management firms (portfolio managers and their sector analysts).

Investor Relations Structure

Structuring an effective Investor Relations team generally depends on numerous factors including the company's philosophy towards the different elements of the overall program and its various constituents. The structure of the group also depends on the company's retail/institutional shareholder mix, the number of sell-side analysts covering the firm, the company's stage of development, the sheer size of the company, its budget and personnel resources, and the overall level of desired and proactive marketing of its stock.

Set by senior management, the philosophy of most companies tends to manifest itself in the highly visible practice of Investor Relations. Some companies tend to be quite conservative in their interaction with the financial community based on a fundamental belief that a very active Investor Relations program is tantamount to hyping the company's stock. Such a conservative approach toward an Investor Relations program would generally result in a minimal program, with minimal communication to Wall Street regardless of the number of an analysts and investors interested in the firm. To the contrary, I believe investor exposure to the company, its management, market position and financials will result in better understanding and decision making on the part of investors and analysts alike. A suitable Investor Relations program will assist in helping investors properly value the firm in public markets and potentially reduce volatility.

Institutional/Retail IR Structure

By focusing on an institutional/retail organizational structure, members of the institutional team focus on serving the needs of the company's major shareholders at firms such as Fidelity and Wellington, as well as the sell-side analysts that are publishing research on a daily basis. The institutional team is generally responsible for managing the quarterly earnings process; conference call; institutional meetings program which includes the annual analyst meeting and support of analyst requests; managing interaction with the listing exchanges such as the New York Stock Exchange or NASDAQ; managing external consultants; interfacing with members of senior management, business development, legal, and the company's public relations staff. One member of the institutional team should have clear oversight for the meetings program and for meeting on a weekly basis to discuss the status of all meeting requests.

The "retail team" focuses its efforts on retail marketing programs such as attending National Association of Investors Corporation (NAIC) regional events; managing the relationship with the company's transfer agent as well as its on-site representatives; interfacing with public relations staff coordinating the annual report; managing the Investor Relations section of the corporate web site; coordinating and managing stockbroker conference calls; and other retail-oriented items.

Administrative staff would be responsible for managing the group's various databases and distribution lists (fax, e-mail, hardcopy); file room; preparation of meetings packages in advance of analyst visits; external event venue selection; and coordinating executive briefing meetings and binders.

This first structure is favored given how clearly the roles and responsibilities are, however members of the retail team may perceive the retail marketing program as less important than the institutional effort given that most of the management interaction will likely take place with institutional activities. Regardless, an active retail shareholder communications program is vital to fostering good shareholder relations and loyalty.

While it is easy to generalize that most publishing sell-side analysts support institutional investors, most of the largest sell-side firms such as Morgan Stanley, Goldman Sachs, and Merrill Lynch also support a large contingent of retail stockbrokers. While these firms are both institutional and retail in nature, many IROs will likely agree that these firms should be considered institutional, given the prominence of these firms' institutional and investment banking strength. There are just a few large sell-side brokerage firms that are largely retail in nature, such as Raymond James and Edward Jones. It is up to the IRO to decide if firms such as these should be managed by the institutional team (by virtue of their sell-side publishing efforts) or managed by the retail team (by virtue of their predominantly or exclusively-retail client base).

To help alleviate issues, the addition of both a separate retail manager, which manages the transfer agent, annual report and other retail-specific items and a meetings program manager, to coordinate all meetings requests, would likely help greatly.

Buy-Side/Sell-Side IR Structure

By focusing on a buy-side/sell-side organizational structure, members of the buy-side team focus on serving the needs of the company's major institutional shareholders - firms such as Fidelity and Wellington - as well as managing marketing programs for all retail shareholders. Under this structure, all publishing sell-side analysts are managed exclusively by the sell-side team.

While the buy-side/sell-side structure sounds fairly straightforward, there are numerous tasks that are more easily organized and managed by virtue of an institutional/retail IR structure.

As an example of the ambiguity that persists under the buy-side/sell-side IR structure, it would be unclear as to whether the buy-side or sell-side team would have a natural responsibility for the Investor Relations meetings program, including coordinating regional management road shows. Such road shows often involve meetings with both the buy-side and the sell-side, possibly evenly divided amongst the two. It is unclear as to which group has responsibility for road show planning, time allocation, schedules, etc. However, most of the meetings would likely be institutional in nature.

In my opinion, while the need for frequent meetings with both the buy-side and the sell-side remain great, both are largely institutional in nature. Hence, the retail/institutional IR structure makes for cleaner delineation of responsibilities. Of course, this problem can be alleviated if separate meetings programs are established for the buy-side team and the sell-side team. However, having separate meetings programs for the buy-side team and the sell-side team are impractical given the limited human resources of typical IR programs. Buy-side road shows and sell-side meetings may inherently be more efficient if managed collectively by the institutional team and staffing it to a higher level.

Other elements of the IR program would involve similar ambiguity, as would deciding which of the two groups have oversight for logistics and content for the annual analyst meeting, at which the entire institutional buy-side and sell-side are invited. As if this level of ambiguity weren't enough, it would also be difficult to determine which group has responsibility for managing the quarterly earnings process, holding results meetings, working on the press release, and scripting and arranging conference call logistics.

Under an institutional/retail IR structure, all of the aforementioned issues would be delegated to the institutional team, as would coordinating major press releases, and developing relevant question and answer documents. As such, if the IRO favors the buy-side/sell-side IR approach, many responsibilities must be clearly assigned to members of the team, and receive keen oversight from the IRO to ensure that they are being efficiently managed.

Regardless, in this approach, significantly more responsibility may remain ambiguous as to which part of the IR team has clear responsibility for certain tasks. As these issues are explored, it is likely that the institutional-retail structure will be preferred.

Reporting to the CFO, Treasurer, or Even The Public Relations Officer

In most companies, the IR team reports directly to the CFO or the company's treasurer. This may or may not seem intuitive, but given the IR team's relationship with the financial analyst community, the function generally rests within the CFO community. While this works quite well, we have seen IR under the company's public relations officer with a dotted-line relationship to the CFO. While this is quite unconventional and most investment bankers would fight tooth and nail to prevent Investor Relations from being too close to the company's PR spin doctors, it actually can work very well – putting first perceptions about PR spin aside. Having a solid-line relationship to the PR community enables a very strong level of support of the PR community, which is very useful. Extensive PR support manifests itself in the form of logistical aid with the annual *retail* shareholder meeting; assistance with the annual *institutional* analyst meeting; script writing for investor conferences; drafting prepared management remarks for the quarterly earnings conference calls; and managing the issuance of press releases and Q&A materials for executive briefing packages. With investors and analysts often meeting with the company's CFO, as lead corporate spokesperson with the financial community, support from the CFO organization is generally a given.

Most traditional reporting structures, in which IR reports into either the company's Treasurer or CFO are quite effective, provided that the necessary linkages are made to Public Relations or appropriate marketing functions. With IR viewed as a very important, and resource constrained, part of the company, resources are generally made available when necessary. The PR community and other parts of the company generally respond quickly to support the needs of the IR team, as the group needs the support of PR for many activities. Working independently, yet through others, members of the IR team can work effectively, as long as its marketing program is embraced by senior management.

One IR Team, Team building Initiatives

With the IRO and the IR team representing the company to the external financial community, the group is often on the forefront of defining its external communications strategies in good times as well as bad. Investors are quick to call the IRO with everything from earnings concerns to rumors about pending acquisitions and won or lost customer contracts. With the assistance of the IRO, the company's response to such unexpected issues often happens in real-time. As such, it is essential that the IR team support each other at each step of the way.

There are a few recommended program elements that can be implemented with relative ease, such as coordinating the annual IR travel outing, quarterly post-earnings gatherings, and holiday events. While it may seem extravagant or unnecessary, the annual IR outing is an important element to maintaining high levels of camaraderie within the close-knit team. Venturing out of the office for some outdoor activities may help refresh the tram for another years' activities. It would not be unheard of during bull markets for the IRO to charter a motor coach to visit a nearby beach or visit a tropical island resort for some rest and relaxation. With corporate sales teams and executives often having team-building excursions, I encourage their use for close-knit and highly stressed IR teams.

7

Institutional Shareholder Marketing Programs

The majority of Investor Relations activities that require management participation will likely involve meetings with institutional investors and analysts. Most of these activities will likely be sponsored by the company, while some will involve participating at various industry sponsored events and conferences. By participating at a combination of company and industry sponsored events, the IR program will reach additional constituents, add credibility to the program, and garner significant goodwill by reaching out with efforts to participate at various investor venues.

While it is vital that the IR effort serve investment community constituents with a hyperactive Investor Relations program, it must at the same time avoid over saturating investors with the same messages or by participating at too many conferences that are targeted at having the participation of identical individuals.

Elements of an effective IR program include annual Management Road shows, Quarterly Earnings Conference Calls, Large Group Topic-specific Conference Calls, Distribution of Marketing Materials, Annual Institutional Analyst Meeting, as well as One-on-One Meetings, Small-group Meetings, and Large Group Meetings.

Institutional "Targeting"

The buy-side is a fairly large community, certainly in comparison to the sell-side, and it would not be uncommon for a publicly traded company to have several hundreds of institutional shareholders. As a result of the breadth of the buy-side community, the IRO must be highly selective of which institutions warrant direct management attention and those that should be served more exclusively by members of the Investor Relations team.

A critical element in the selection process for deciding how best to prioritize IR and management resources is often referred to as shareholder "targeting." Formal targeting efforts should be done on a monthly basis, including identification of each institutional shareholder's net position in your company's securities, their additional share purchase potential, and net changes in their holdings over the last month, three months, six months and year. Additionally, the purchase potential of prospective new shareholders should be determined at the same time, particularly if their firms' primary investment style matches the profile of your company. Furthermore, another key element to effective shareholder targeting involves determining the amount of shares that each institution holds in peer companies, the market sector, and the broader market. All of which yields useful and potentially actionable intelligence.

This ongoing effort may be the basis for selecting particular firms for participation in your company's meetings program. While buy-side shareholder targeting is often the focus of many IR programs, it can also be done with the sell-side, in an effort to generate additional research coverage on the company. While many large companies have more than ample research coverage, many smaller ones desire additional research coverage and seek to attract the interest of various research analysts.

Chapter 7: Institutional Shareholder Marketing Programs

Company-Sponsored Events

I. Regional Roadshows

Effective IR programs will generally have members of senior management meet with major shareholders or potential shareholders in their respective home offices, approximately once per year.

While these in-person meetings can be formally apart of a formal IR road show, management travel schedules often bring them to various major cities for events such as employee gatherings, customer meetings, factory visits, board meetings, philanthropy efforts, meetings with union representatives and for numerous other corporate activities. Accordingly, the periodic attainment of executive business travel schedules from executive secretaries, administrative assistants or executive assistants can help the IRO coordinate shareholder meetings that take advantage of existing travel plans. More than likely, company executives are more than happy to leverage their travel schedules for an additional meeting or two. This certainly has been my experience.

IR coordination for these types of visits can be limited to hosting a sole meeting at a major shareholder's location or involve sponsoring a breakfast meeting with various investors at a nearby hotel. Larger shareholders will more likely expect an on-site visit so that the firm's various portfolio managers can attend with ease.

There is no substitute for the CEO, CFO and other senior members of management for meetings with portfolio managers at companies such as Alliance Capital, Janus and Fidelity in their main offices. However, in many cases, the analysts at these firms are more than happy to host the IRO alone to compare notes on the company and the industry and to involve a number of portfolio managers in the meeting as well. While regional road shows are an essential element to an active Investor Relations marketing program, members of the Investor Relations team are welcome to execute them independently as well. Outside the United States, a visit from the IRO, which generally includes a formal presentation, by and large is as welcome as a visit from the company's CEO. Likely European financial centers of interest will be London, Paris, Zurich and Geneva.

II. Quarterly Earnings Conference Calls

Management teams typically discuss the company's quarterly earnings results on conference calls with the financial community. While some senior executives prefer to speak from presentation slides and talking points, at large corporations management remarks are generally pre-scripted by both the company's public relations speechwriters and IR team, in order to focus on the most important topics that will likely be on the minds of investors. An interactive Q&A session typically follows prepared management remarks.

While conference calls are not required, many smaller companies do without them entirely and instead handle investor inquiries on an as needed basis following the issuance of their press release. With volumes of investors to manage, larger companies generally opt to host a single call with several hundred participants in order to address the bulk of investor questions. Regardless, even micro capitalized companies should consider providing a conference call to offer as many opportunities as possible for investors to have access to management. Naturally, investors will also scour over your company's Federal filings, including 10Qs, 10Ks and 8K/As.

To truly differentiate your company in the earnings season, we encourage IROs to consider a focus topic each quarter that enables the financial community to not just understand the details of the quarter's earnings release, but also to focus their attention on a special topic. As examples, the addition of the president of a division offering a look at a new technology; provide an up-close look at certain European operations; offer a post-merger integration update of a recent acquisition; or even a presentation by a notable customer to demonstrate the value your company has provided.

Cisco's Investor Relations program makes insightful topics a routine part of its conference calls. The company also makes a point of discussing what was better and worse than expected during the quarter. Anything insightful is of interest to investors. By going the extra mile by including such topics and insights, the result is a significantly improved conference call and a greater understanding of the company for investors than would otherwise be achieved. Any area that you are particularly proud of can be showcased in this quarterly opportunity to leverage investors' carving out the time to focus on your company. Leverage the time that investors carve out.

Conference Call Duration

In our experience, the most "pleasant" duration of quarterly conference calls for investors is approximately 30 minutes allocated for prepared remarks with an additional 20 to 50 minutes allocated to questions and answers. Accordingly, these calls last approximately 50 minutes to 80 minutes. There is no ideal conference call length, although most companies plan for about one hour and reserve sufficient conference call ports for an additional 30 minutes to be on the safe side, in case the call overruns for an unanticipated reason.

There are some very well regarded companies that allow their calls to last longer. While these conference calls tend to become less interesting as they approach an hour in length, they do serve a useful purpose. They can provide each person on the call with an opportunity to ask questions, making all participants feel valued and obtaining the satisfaction of having their voice heard by management. The value of this is quite significant for sell side analysts, as they tend to constantly feel pressure to be visible, ask questions and publish research. However, on the downside, call participants will often disconnect the call before it has officially concluded and executives have had their final opportunity to add closing remarks and commentary.

It is recommended that longer calls be utilized in an effort to ensure that analysts have an opportunity to ask as many questions as possible, to the benefit of all on the call and for those who wish to gain the maximum benefit by listening to its conclusion.

Post Conference Call Follow-up Discussions

Immediately after the large-group conference call concludes, it is often desirable for the IRO to join the CFO in hosting a small number, perhaps just three or four, follow-up conversations with the buy-side analysts of the company's largest institutional shareholders. These calls can be scheduled for just fifteen minutes each to address any specific concerns.

Internet Web Casting

As quarterly earnings conference calls are quite expensive to host due to the per-minute rates charged by telecom providers, Web casting is particularly economical. Although asking real-time questions is not generally possible when logging into the call from the Internet, many participants will take advantage of a corporate Web cast. If presentation materials are to accompany management's talk, those with broadband Internet access will dial into the call real-time and download related presentations and press releases from the company's Web site. Given the great number of individual investors that follow stocks, it is quite easy and inexpensive to invite them to listen to the call in this manner.

The ability to log into the Web cast replay from anywhere and replay the recording is particularly useful. At a minimum, conference calls broadcast over the web may be useful from an SEC Regulation Fair Disclosure (Reg. FD) point of view, depending on your company's interpretation of the requirements for compliance. Conference calls should be made available immediately upon conclusion of the call and available for at least a few weeks. Ideally they can be archived permanently on the company's Web page next to its associated earnings press release and presentation material.

III. Large Group Topic-specific Conference Calls

While quarterly earnings calls are an essential staple of most IR programs, many companies do not generally host separate topic-specific calls, with the exception of major acquisition announcements. Planned topic-specific conference calls can easily be woven into the IR program once or twice per year, and are designed to highlight various corporate divisions, products or new technologies. At any company, there are likely to be a few pressing areas of interest about your company that the financial community would like to hear significantly more about.

Held outside the normal earnings season, coordinating these calls, often with operational management, the company gains an opportunity to showcasing any area of the business so desired with the full attention of the financial community. With publishing sell-side analysts somewhat less fatigued than they are during the normal earnings season, a number of research notes are likely to be issued as a result of your effort. Additionally, the buy-side will enjoy learning about a new part of the company, clear of the stress and financial modeling that occurs during earnings season and after earnings conference calls. If a particular individual is interested in the topic, they can take advantage of the call real time or listen to a replay.

Effective topic-specific conference calls need not be hosted by senior executives, but rather can be hosted by division level executives and vice presidents. Naturally, the IRO must feel very comfortable with the person or persons representing the company on such operational calls and that the featured executives will not speak to broader company issues, such as its ability to meet earnings estimates, the likelihood of potential acquisitions, stock-splits or other corporate matters. It is often best to keep these calls to a product nature, discussing for example the benefits of a new technology or a recent new product or services development. Providing the investment community with the opportunity to participate on theses calls provides the type of transparency that is highly consistent with serving the investment community well. I highly encourage hosting them given the impact they can have at elevating your IR program.

IV. Annual Flagship Institutional Analyst Meeting

Most public companies host a flagship institutional analyst meeting annually for members of the institutional buy- and sell- side communities. Many companies enjoy hosting these meetings at their corporate headquarters location, although when they do, the event tends to take on a life of its own. We have seen companies go to great lengths, including setting up the equivalent of a small-scale trade show on site with dozens of product demonstrations and technical experts.

For large group meetings, it is worthwhile to consider the addition of select product demos and breakout sessions with members of the company's operational management or technical community. Lunch tables can include having various executives join tables, where they can get exposure to the investment community. An executive-hosted reception can take place either before or after the meeting. Some companies take the annual institutional shareholder meeting as an opportunity to expand the effort into a fairly prolonged, even weeklong event to separately host customers, suppliers, industry analysts and the media. I encourage participation at the company's institutional analyst meeting by select customers, with whom your company is a valued partner and can offer insightful testimonials. The uniqueness of each company and its industry can provide quite a few interesting meeting segments.

It is important that the complexity of such a meeting NOT be a factor in the decision of whether to host one. Accordingly, while large companies typically present themselves to the financial community with many senior and operational executives, simply presenting your company's CFO and CEO for 45-minutes each, followed by a 45 minute Q&A session will likely be enough to cover most of the issues facing the company and the industry.

The logistical details required in hosting an all-day or multi-day analyst meeting are numerous and can expand exponentially as the event expands. These details range from coordinating executive presentation materials; completing executive briefing packages; hosting the final executive preparatory meeting the evening before for the event to review logistics; assembling analyst binders and meeting materials; coordinating breakout sessions; and arranging car service for attendees.

Analyst meetings such as this are important elements to your IR program and, if possible, should be done either at your corporate headquarters or in New York City, which is also very convenient to individuals in the financial centers of Boston, Baltimore and Philadelphia. Additionally, with access to several international airports, members of the European financial community will have minimal flight time and change in time zone when traveling to New York.

While some companies may opt to decline hosting institutional shareholder meetings during challenging times, IROs and senior managers should be reminded that consistency is often a significant factor to the investment community. Lack of consistency is generally viewed as a negative and may impact investor perceptions of the company. As such, retrenching your IR program and skipping elements of the program during some of the more challenging times is not a viable option in my view. It is far more important to have consistent communication with the financial community at all times, even if the news could be better than it is, than to selectively add and subtract elements to your program during good, and challenging, times.

Having an opportunity to discuss any current market updates and information is useful over the long term for your company's credibility, even if it may appear less than helpful over the short term. In fact, some companies increase their large group meeting efforts to twice per year during challenging times. I encourage all companies to consider a second in-person institutional shareholder meeting during their most difficult of times.

As with quarterly conference calls, these large group meetings are increasingly broadcast live over the Internet. In this way, retail investors have access to the contents of the in-person institutional meeting. If attended by the media, participation is often limited to listen-only participation. Regardless, the inclusion of the media may lead to desirable and broad media exposure of the event. Numerous sell-side analyst notes will be published as well and their commentary should be sent to senior management as soon as possible.

V. One-on-One Meetings, Small Group Meetings and Large Group Meetings

One-on-one meetings represent the most personal interaction that members of the financial community will have with senior management and the IRO. They are extremely worth the extensive time involved in hosting them and should be a top priority and a very active element of most IR programs. One-on-one meetings allow both management and investors to look each other in the eye and get to know each other's personal styles.

Small group meetings can be extremely effective elements of the firm's Investor Relations program. These meetings can be held at the company's headquarters or in major cities, either as part of formal road shows or otherwise. Bringing a small number of investors and analysts together, often over breakfast or lunch, can be highly useful elements of the IR program. Small group meetings are among the most valuable vehicles to address a long line of constituents' requests for meeting with executives. Rotating management members into a corporate dining room to provide visiting members of the financial community with an overview of the company's major divisions for meetings with management is an effective way to utilize management time, particularly after an IPO or other event when management exposure is high. A combination of technical individuals and division presidents makes for quite a productive set of meetings.

Large group meetings sponsored by companies are typically restricted to the company's annual institutional shareholder meetings. While the company's annual institutional shareholder and analyst meeting is clearly the flagship of all IR meetings, there are other opportunities to bring together large groups of investors, such as at major industry trade shows. I strongly encourage all IROs to consider expanded meetings activities at the largest and most important trade shows and industry conferences.

A collection of one-on-one and small group meetings periodically in New York, Boston and other financial centers can be quite productive whether or not that are separated or combined into mini-road shows. Sorties to nearby financial centers for meetings with members of the sell-side and buy-side can be easily coordinated and should be held as frequently as possible.

VI. Distribution of Corporate Marketing Materials

Many companies have vast amounts of public information available in the form of in –house customer or employee magazines, product brochures and other interesting materials. As many topics of interest to the investment community routinely pass IRO desks, it would be wise to consider distribution of these materials periodically to buy-side and sell-side analysts alike, if they are suitable for such external distribution.

One of the best approaches to utilizing your company's existing marketing materials would be to select an appropriate document and simply send copies to the company's top 100 institutional buy-side analysts and all of your sell-side analysts, with a cover letter from the IRO. The mind-share that can be attained from distribution of such materials may be substantial and the effort to do is minimal. Distribution of the company's annual report should be routine in either hardcopy or electronic format.

Any document being considered for distribution to a select number of individuals must not be material in nature from a legal perspective. As with all IR decisions, consult with legal counsel to ensure compliance with all applicable laws and regulations.

If your company doesn't have items that are broad enough to be useful with the financial community, driving the creation of an appropriate "product and services" catalog might be useful for distribution. Items for distribution can be in catalog format, industry-specific wall posters, or burned into electronic format onto CDs or Adobe PDF files.

Industry Sponsored Conferences and Meetings

Sell-side analysts also sponsor their own conferences and meetings, bringing together the members of management from various companies directly with *their* institutional buy-side trading clients - analysts and portfolio managers. Of course, many of these individuals are clients of other sell-side brokerage firms and are often your very own shareholders and prospective shareholders. As an example, a broker-dealer may hold its annual two-day Communications Industry Conference in New York City or its annual Energy Services Conference in Houston. The brokerage firm's buy-side clients are invited to attend the conference in order to gain exposure to the management teams of companies under its coverage, as well as to various private companies and other industry players.

Typically, the broker-dealer's event marketing communications team coordinates most logistical details and manages corporate and investor invitations and participation. Companies are invited to participate in large-group presentations, including keynotes or panel discussions, breakout-room meetings and various one-on-one meetings. Companies that participate generally take advantage of all three venues when traveling to such conferences. With the majority of logistical details handled by the broker-dealer, very few details require coordination by the company's IR team, making participation easy for management (and the IRO).

While the broker-dealer may coordinate all logistical details, keen oversight should be taken with regard to any one-on-one meetings offered. The IRO will likely need to be involved on some level to help select which firms are invited for participation and to avoid having meetings with major clients of the brokerage firm that may not truly be interested in your company. Often, hedge funds will seek such meetings to glean insights on potential acquisition candidates, while small cap growth fund managers may seek insight on some of your smaller competitors, rather that seeking to truly understand your company. Topics of conversation at meetings should be focused primarily on your company.

Given that corporate participation at a limited number of sell-side conferences is possible, IROs at large companies often negotiate keynote engagements or preferred presentation times for their senior management. By choosing to participate, the relationships between all parties involved often strengthen as a result.

It is very important not to participate in either too many nor too few sell-side sponsored conferences each year, and to be careful not to saturate the buy-side that attends with content that is all too familiar and is used too often. As many investors are firmly apart of the normal conference circuit, frequently updating content and adding new areas of focus is extremely important. It is also critical to reinforce the same general corporate messages and themes. Striking a balance between having ample new content and reinforcing overall corporate messages and themes is a difficult task that should be balanced carefully. Consider having presentation material refer to long-standing financial metrics and updating progress toward such goals.

Selecting which conferences to participate at annually should be based on such factors including the strength of the sell-side franchise offering the conference, the distance from the close of the quarter, and the number of times that the company presented at in the past. Ideally it would be best to select conferences that begin just after the close of the quarter and never during an earnings blackout period, which often begin mid-way through the third month of a quarter. While avoiding conference participation during blackout periods, it is often possible to have technical subject matter experts present on various issues, as long as their formal responsibilities are far removed from corporate results and issues. Targeting approximately four to six sell-side conferences per year is generally adequate for most companies, although doing more is often helpful to reinforce ongoing corporate themes and messages, clarifying anticipated corporate announcements, and focusing investor attention on certain corporate divisions and management members.

While there are also various professional societies and investor forums that will invite the company to various venues, by far the most influential fund managers and analysts are gathered at company-sponsored events and certain sell-side conferences. Select participation at independent societies and investing forums with great care.

Leverage The Sell-side "Morning Call"

Sell-side analysts at broker-dealers typically present their views on industry developments and summaries of the recent research notes each morning, usually beginning at 7:30am. The morning call, as it is known, generally lasts until about 8:30 to 9:15, during which time the firm's sales force has an opportunity to question analysts about their recent research notes, as well as current views, recommendations and earnings estimates. Calls at larger brokerage firms can certainly last longer, but in general, members of the sales force that are in attendance generally desire making outbound calls to the buy-side before normal trading begins at 9:30am.

While many sales calls run long, given analysts' general desire to talk at fair length and express the depth of their knowledge, there are many days when news flow and analyst participation on the call is light, typically on Mondays and Fridays. Management or Investor Relations participation on morning calls represent a substantial opportunity to generate additional corporate exposure, in a highly unconventional but useful way. By participating on the morning call, management teams can deliver short presentations directly to a sell-side sales force. While the firm's sell-side analyst may have certain opinions on the company's stock, the sales force generally welcomes insight from management directly.

If a morning call has a large number of participants on a given day, coordinators of the morning meeting – typically the research-sales liaison and equity research director - will gladly reassemble the sales force later in the morning, during lunch or just after the close of the market. In that event, your presentation will likely be a topic of discussion for the next day's sales calls made to buy-side portfolio managers and analysts.

From my experience, participating on the morning call is a very under-utilized vehicle for management to gain exposure to the Street. Generally, all morning-call presentations and meetings held in the morning meeting room are recorded and the calls are distributed live globally to the firm's regional sales force in overseas locations such as London, Paris, Zurich and Geneva as well as in major United States cities such as Boston, San Francisco, Chicago, Atlanta and elsewhere. It is important to note that buy-side analysts and portfolio managers, clients of the brokerage firm, may also be dialing into the morning call for a review of major issues impacting the markets.

Ascertaining time on the sell-side morning call is a refreshing experience for management members and the gingerly treatment and respect that most buy-side analysts and portfolio managers offer is not often a characteristic of some members of a typical brokerage sales force. By gathering management together with the sales force in the morning meeting room, the IRO and management team will be provided with a sense of the working environment of sell-side analysts and a truly invaluable experience. Be forewarned, but do not be deterred.

Sell-side Sponsored Institutional Marketing Efforts

Sell-side analysts periodically ask IROs to allow them to coordinate meetings with institutional shareholders and buy-side analysts. While it may be tempting to avail of the logistical ease afforded by these offers, from a purely company point of view, it is best to plan the far majority of IR meetings directly between the firm and its institutional shareholders.

By coordinating such meetings, the analyst may validate his or her expertise and stature in the industry by appearing close to management. However, in my opinion, marketing side-by-side and frequently with sell-side analysts is not likely desirable from a corporate point of view. From an analyst point of view, however, it may be quite desirable.

Blast E- Mail, V-Mail and Faxes

Institutional shareholders generally receive sell-side analyst research notes by email, paper mail and fax. They also often receive blast voice mails from the sell-side in relation to ratings changes, earnings results and general industry updates. Effective Investor Relations programs can also take advantage of the latest technology and useful tools to fine-tune elements of their marketing program. Communicating with members of the investment community can be done in a variety of creative ways. As an example, blast voice mails can also be sent from the IRO to both the investment community and/ or members of senior management to announce conference calls, earnings release dates, large group meetings or to simply reinforce information from press releases.

8

Retail Shareholder Marketing Programs

The majority of a company's Investor Relations budget may be spent on supporting a vast numbers of individual investors that own the company's stock, including fees related to managing the transfer agent's shareholder administration program, managing international call center staff and distributing the annual proxy material and annual report.

Given the influence and high visibility of institutional sell-side and buy-side analysts and portfolio managers, it is possible for a retail shareholder program to fall neglected. Managing an effective and hyperactive retail shareholder marketing program is also critical.

While hosting the annual retail shareholder meeting and distributing the company's annual report are the two flagship methods by which the retail shareholder community is generally reached, there are many programs that IROs can use to enhance their visibility with the vast retail shareholder base. Among these approaches is participation at NAIC conferences, distributing corporate fact kits to thousands of retail stockbrokers and hosting conference calls - directly with retail stockbrokers.

Stockbroker Satellite Broadcasts and Conference Calls

While investment firms such as Merrill Lynch have many highly-ranked sell-side analysts and a large institutional sales force marketing analyst research to buy-side clients, they also have a very large number of retail stockbrokers. The firm's stockbrokers, numbering several thousand in size, are highly influential with their high net worth retail investor clients. Retail brokerage firms often distribute company-specific and industry research summaries appropriate to retail clientele, which are often somewhat more high-level in nature than the research reports that are distributed to the institutional sales force and institutional investment community.

Regardless, by having members of your management participate in satellite-based, or even simple teleconferences, vast numbers of stockbrokers can be reached directly by your management and these interactions can be quite helpful to aiding their understanding of your company. These broadcasts and conference calls are often facilitated by the firm's sell-side analyst, which knows your company particularly well. We encourage these interviews to take place periodically as part of an active marketing program to effectively reach the retail shareholder community. Stockbrokers can be instructed on how to acquire the company's most recent investor kits and corporate fact sheets for distribution to their high net worth clients.

Retail Investor Kits and Corporate Fact Sheets

Retail investors, like their institutional counterparts, can benefit from receiving packages of information that contain materials on the company, its executives, financial performance, market, and other information. IROs are encouraged to have these materials updated and stocked by members of their staff on quarterly basis and have a supply of them on hand to distribute directly in response to various retail investor inquiries.

Some corporations retain a distribution center to assemble and maintain a supply of these investor kits. The retail marketing effort will note how investors can receive the latest corporate fact kit, including the latest annual reports, fact sheets, press releases and newsletters. By having a distribution center centrally manage the assembly and shipment of corporate investor kits, retail stockbrokers, for example, can order 25 or 50 of these kits for distribution to their retail clients.

Even if your investor kit contains a laminated corporate fact sheet, a few quarterly press releases, an annual report, and other materials, the effort can go a long way at helping investors make an informed decision about the company.

The "Own Your Share of America" Program

If your company has a strong retail following, participation in the "Own Your Share of America" program may also be of interest to you. The program is also sponsored by the non-profit National Association of Investors Corporation (NAIC), which promotes general equity investing principles such as the benefits of investing in a periodic fashion and the value of having a diversified portfolio. The NAIC has approximately 350 corporate sponsors include AT&T, Lucent Technologies, Bristol-Myers Squibb, McDonalds, The Walt Disney Company, Wal-Mart, Whirlpool, Tiffany, Texaco, and many other well-known corporations. Full details of the program can be found at www.oysa.org.

National Association of Investors Corporation (NAIC) Events

Not all companies utilize NAIC regional events as vehicles to attract and retain retail shareholders, however we strongly encourage their use. If your company has a strong retail shareholder base, joining the non-profit NAIC may be a valued resource for the IRO. Participation at various NAIC events, which take place in many regions of the country, will certainly help raise your company's profile with individual investors. Direct participation at approximately two to six major NAIC events should be sufficient for most companies, depending on its size and percentage of retail shareholders.

Generally, participation at NAIC events requires at least two to three members of your team, and possible a fourth. While at NAIC events, members of the IR team can often make a formal presentation to those in attendance as well as staff a kiosk booth. While staffing a kiosk is far from glamorous, it is an opportunity to discuss the company's products and services, recap recent earnings news, and distribute annual reports, quarterly newsletters, shareholder kits and various corporate gift items.

It would be wise to preview an NAIC event before officially participating, as the vast range of corporate kiosks and marketing approaches will be quite varied and interesting. If you decide to participate in these flagship retail events, your company will likely need to purchase a kiosk, store it and ship it to each regional event. Corporate participation at these events is very time consuming, given the travel requirements, set-up time and strain of working the show floor for great periods of time. The resource requirement of participation at these events may make the cost-benefit ratio prohibitively high.

Quarterly Newsletter Mailings

As some individual investors may not yet have broadband Internet access or easy access to quarterly 10Q filings, the quarterly mailing of an Investor Relations newsletter can be quite useful to informing them of quarterly news items. Consider mailing a few pages with a summary of your quarterly earnings press release, with focuses on additional areas of investor interest. The company's transfer agent can distribute these easily once printed. Such newsletters can be distributed via e-mail if the shareholder's preference is to receive electronic format.

Annual Report

While typically handled by the company's public relations team, the annual report represents a key element in the retail Investor Relations program. Accordingly, members of the IR team are often consulted on the overall theme of the document, its messages, content and design. Annual reports can be very expensive and smaller companies, as well as larger cost conscious ones, tend to craft it from the annual Federal filing, the Form 10K.

Often a color inset within a few introductory and summary pages surrounds the Form 10K and this combination collectively makes up the company's annual report. I agree with the cost conscious approach as a highly effective one and that the full-color and elaborate reports that were common in the 1990s bull market are unnecessary.

Annual reports make for great handouts and distributions at NAIC events, annual meetings and other retail – or institutional - venues. Sending copies of the annual report to institutional analysts that may not be shareholders is also likely a good idea. Additionally, annual report distribution can be via e-mail if the shareholder's preference is to receive electronic distribution.

Annual Retail Shareholder Meeting

The company's annual shareholder meeting is generally the preeminent meeting for the retail shareholder community. The structure of the annual meeting is generally to present the year's financial results and to discuss topic of current interest. These events are often modestly attended in relation to the size of your retail shareholder base, but hosting one is a required element of being a public company. As retail investors that attend generally get right to the point, be prepared for very direct Q&A sessions and a fair amount of media coverage.

The Corporate Home Page

Increasingly, individual investors are becoming ever proficient at navigating the Web for information on your company, competitors, industry data and broader financial market data. With common Web tools, shareholders can sign up for inclusion into the company's mass e-mail list, so that they can be instantly notified of the issuance of corporate press releases. With Web-based tools, there would be little if any maintenance required to administer such services, easing the responsibility for the company's IR team. We encourage IROs to put as much public data on the Web, including information on:

- Annual retail shareholder meeting;
- Retail stockbroker events;
- Regional NAIC events;
- Press releases, quarterly newsletters and annual reports;
- Web cast information for earnings conference calls and the annual institutional analyst meeting;

- Upcoming sell-side industry conferences; and
- Corporate presentations and technical white papers.

Live Internet Video and Audio Web Casting

Anytime the corporation discloses material information, it important to make this information available to all investors immediately. In order to satisfy disclosure rules, live Internet Web casting of major Investor Relations activities such as quarterly conference calls and presentations at sell-side conferences, may be acceptable. Web casting over the Internet makes content available real-time to all interested parties, including individual investors. But Web casting has equal benefits to members of the media, employees, industry analysts, suppliers, customers and competitors alike.

Many companies archive conference call replays and educational video segments on their corporate Web site along side press releases, corporate presentations, white papers and other documents of interest. The ability for investors to replay audio and video casts at their convenience is particularly useful.

Targeted Corporate Advertising

With corporate advertising and branding programs also reaching investors, corporate advertisements programs can also be effectively placed in magazines and other periodicals that cater to either individual investors, such as Worth and Money, or broader periodicals such as Business Week or the Wall Street Journal.

Advertising of all forms can greatly reinforce a company's brand and the key facts about the company. As an example, Hewlett Packard's public relations team led a vast advertising campaign after the company announced its intention to merge with Compaq, detailing the merits of the transaction. While the proxy fight was heated indeed, the advertising campaign reinforced the company's vision that the merger held many merits. Regardless of the scale of the program, advertising will help effectively reach both your retail and institutional shareholder constituencies.

Managing Retail Shareholders

Most IR teams do not have sufficient resources to manage the influx of calls and letters from vast numbers of individual investors. As a result, most incoming communication from retail shareholders will be routed to the company's transfer agent where they can be addressed by a larger support staff. Those shareholders that reach the company directly will need to be addressed by the company's executive response center and assigned to a specific representative to monitor the handling of the issue in order to have the issue resolved in a satisfactory and timely manner. Most retail shareholders will contact the transfer agent with issues ranging from questions on how to purchase shares directly from the company, how to report lost stock certificates, respond to proxy materials or odd-lot tender offers, and how to transfer securities upon the death of the beneficial owner.

The Transfer Agent

The transfer agent manages various call centers that are staffed with employees that answer questions from individual shareholders on a variety of issues. It is essential that IRO meet regularly with representatives of its transfer agent, including those individuals at the call center, where most basic questions are directed. While there, you will be able to meet the individuals that answer calls and letters from shareholders regard the transfer of securities and other basic transfer and voting related issues.

While call centers are often characterized by having high employee turnover, meeting with the staff them regularly can be a boost to their morale and assist in their understanding of the company they are supporting. It may be desirable to listen to a few incoming calls from your shareholders to gain an appreciation for what is being done by the transfer agent's representatives to provide them with feedback. It is also encouraged to watch for investor complaints against transfer agent representatives and take appropriate action if necessary. Staffers at the call center represent your company and it is essential that your shareholders receive accurate information and are treated in a respectful and proper manner.

It is also strongly encouraged that penalties be imposed on the transfer agent if adequate quality levels are not maintained. As an example, a company's agreement with its transfer agent might stipulate that if average shareholder wait time exceeds two minutes or if turnover and absenteeism become excessive, that certain penalties be imposed. Further, consider additional penalties can be applied if a certain number of calls are directed to the corporate executive response center or are received by the management team directly because of improper handling, dissemination of incorrect information or arise from specific complaints about the transfer agent and its call center staff. The company's transfer agent should be held accountable in the event that issues are not handled or resolved in a satisfactory and timely manner.

In relation to specific IR activities, the transfer agent generally distributes shareholder voting materials, proxy materials and annual reports. As an IRO, you may inherit many established consultants and services providers, such as your transfer agent. It is important to note that corporations, even very large ones, do occasionally change transfer agents.

The On-site Transfer Agent Representative

If possible, I strongly recommend that at least one employee from your transfer agent be on-site in your corporate IR offices to field any inquiries that may be directed to senior executives. The on-site representative from the transfer agent can also respond to e-mails received from the company's Web page, messages left on the general IR voice mailbox and letters directed to senior management. Additionally, the on-site representative can be responsible for answering transfer related questions received at the corporate offices, informing the IRO of weekly call volumes, dropped call rates, post-call survey results and the status of various distributions, including the annual report and proxy materials. The on-site rep will also function as an effective liaison between the IRO and the transfer agent, ensuring that important issues are expedited and resolved in a satisfactory manner.

One innovative approach to ensuring that the transfer agent is doing its job in a satisfactory would be to indicate that a cash penalty be remitted to the company if your senior executives receive more than a certain number of communications regarding basic transfer-agent issues. The IR staff should regularly meet with members of the call center and ensure that they are comfortable answering basic questions about the company and that ample materials are available to be sent to shareholders with questions.

Odd-lot Share Repurchase Programs and Direct Purchase Programs (DPPs)

It is highly recommended that the IR effort include an ongoing analysis of the company's retail shareholders and the number that hold very few shares, such as fewer than 50 or 100. When odd-lot holdings reach undesirable levels, the company can implement a low-cost share repurchase program to reduce the number of small positions by buying back the shares held directly.

Additionally, the company can inform holders of odd-lot positions that it has a direct stock purchase plan (DPP) which allows them to buy additional shares directly from the company for a very small transaction fee. With many direct stock purchase plans, the transaction may be executed instantly as with on-line brokerage accounts, but rather when the purchase or sale instructions are received in the mail. During this processing time, the value of the stock on the open may rise or fall to the shareholder's advantage or disadvantage. With the transaction cost of most discount brokerages approaching $5 to $10 per trade, "buying direct" is not likely to result in significant transactional savings. Regardless, some individuals prefer to deal directly with the company itself and not hold securities in a separate brokerage account.

With the ongoing cost of printing annual reports, mailing proxy statements and otherwise administering shareholder programs ever increasing, administering them can be more cost-effective by implementing a variety of cost-reduction initiatives.

Dividend Reinvestment Plans (DRIPs)

Many individuals feel strongly about reinvesting dividends that they receive from the company, in order to compound their investment growth and ascertain the true value of their initial investment. Many others prefer to reinvest their dividends elsewhere or outright spend their quarterly dividend check. It is desirable to offer investors the option to reinvesting their dividends unless the cost and complexity associated with administering your firm's DRIP is prohibitive.

Corporate Gifts

Inexpensive corporate gifts items, such as corporate Investor Relations information magnets, coffee mugs, pens and other items often make excellent gifts for retail investors. Marketing to retail investors at regional NAIC events generally involves trinkets of all sorts.

9

Strategic Elements of Investor Relations

Execute Against The Annual Investor Relations Plan

Given the continual activity associated with managing an Investor Relations program, many IROs pass on development of an annual plan for the upcoming year. In the course of documenting end-of-year accomplishments and preparing personal objectives for the upcoming one, it is often useful for the IRO to take the opportunity to develop a more detailed IR marketing plan for the year ahead. From my perspective, the time will be well worth the effort.

By updating organizational charts and updating the existing framework for anticipated activities for the year ahead, the IRO will galvanize management's commitment and support for the IR program. Additionally, as they are requested to represent the company at analyst conferences, trade show, one-on-one meetings, and conference calls, management will be reminded of the dedicated planning effort of the IRO and best understand how he or she fits into the upcoming year's program. Adjustments can be made based on specific management feedback. The annual IR plan should be distributed to only a few individuals such as the CEO, CFO, Controller, Treasurer and Corporate Secretary and should receive substantial input from both the retail and institutional IR programs.

Earnings Guidance

To Provide, Or Not Provide Guidance

Some public companies have eliminated providing the analyst community with earnings guidance entirely, even though such companies likely have internal outlook projections. We view the lack of any guidance as a disservice to both the analyst community and the company itself and caution against joining this growing bandwagon. While companies may likely have less exposure if they miss analyst earnings expectations, the analyst community will still need to create highly-detailed financial models and publish revenue and earnings estimates even if the company provides no guidance whatsoever. With or without corporate guidance, earnings estimates by analysts will be consolidated into consensus figures by the likes of Zacks and FirstCall. On earnings day, the company will have either met, exceeded or missed published consensus analyst earnings figures. By providing no guidance whatsoever, the company may be inflicting volatility into its equity trading needlessly.

It should strongly be considered that if visibility permits, some guidance should be provided to aid the investment community in understanding corporate expectations. However, we recommend providing the analyst community with a moderate or wide range of corporate expectations, as opposed to a more narrow range.

Having A Wide Range of Earnings Estimates

In many ways, it is helpful to have a wide range of analyst estimates on the company's stock. By having a variety of estimates, when the company meets consensus expectations, it will meet certain analyst expectations and likely disappoint some at the same time. If the company's earnings guidance is highly specific, analysts may adopt it with little deviation. Hence, if the company meets or exceeds expectations, it will likely have many supporters, but if it misses consensus, it will likely not have many.

Responding to Rumors

For good reasons, companies often have very clear policies of not responding to rumors and speculation. In some cases however, the company is faced with a difficult situation whereby rumors are circulating in the market and these rumors appear to be markedly driving the share price either up or down. Under most situations, stating to members of the media that the company does not respond to rumors and speculation is ample, as it is a very fair response given that the company has no material information to announce.

However, an aspect that may complicate the issue is a desire, if not responsibility, to protect shareholder value. If the company's stock is declining significantly based on clearly unfounded rumors, with no possible basis in fact, it may decide to refute the rumor. As examples, the company can press release a reiteration of its comfort level with prior earnings guidance or otherwise deny that the company is going to miss consensus earnings estimates, acquire a company, etcetera.

An executive interview with a wire reporter at Reuters or Dow Jones Newswires is a very effective way to respond to these rumors. Refuting a rumor, however, sets a precedent. And if the company responds to a rumor that it is not expecting to miss earnings for a particular quarter, it may seem logical that it will respond again if there are such rumors in the future. A lack of a response by the company may be perceived as validating the rumor as true, whether or not this is an accurate or inaccurate assumption. This is a difficult situation because, as a company, it is not generally beneficial to respond to all rumors, true or untrue. Announcements should generally be made at a time that they company selects and when all the details are finalized and ready for prime time.

When To Pre-announce Earnings

To some degree, it can be argued whether or not companies have a formal responsibility to pre-announce earnings results that will not meet analyst expectations, or rather to announce the disappointing results on its regularly scheduled earnings date. However, the general compulsion is to release any material information as soon as it is known. Accordingly, if a company is going to miss earnings estimates by a material margin, the company's counsel may recommend that the company pre-announce the results in advance. A central question is how wide of an earnings, or revenue, miss is considered material.

Individuals that purchase the company's stock during the period of time that the company learns that it will likely miss expectations by a material margin and the time that earnings are released may argue that they would have not bought the stock if they knew what the company knew at the time. Hence the need for a pre-announcement of negative earnings results as soon as such information is believed to be likely. However, setting the precedent of pre-announcements may lead investors to believe that in the absence of such an announcement by a certain date that the company has made its financial numbers or at least has not missed by a "material" margin.

There are also times when a company will chose to pre-announce positive earnings results, although the instances are clearly far fewer. As an example, if a company's stock is declining on rumors of a negative pre-announcement, the company's desire to protect shareholder value may drive such an announcement. By deciding to pre-announce again, the mere presence of unfounded rumors may result in action on the part of the corporation. Again, doing so sets a precedent and any action needs to be well thought.

The "CEO Factor"

While Cisco CEO John Chambers remains an icon of excellence in corporate communication and management, his participation at countless customer and analyst meetings has earned him many accolades with the investment community. Long after Chambers retires from Cisco, his legacy will live on for driving best-in-class processes throughout the company. His participation at analyst meetings, tradeshows and with customers represents role model behavior for CEOs of all publicly traded companies. While some would have argued that Chambers is so visible, his personal "currency" became diluted, I don't believe this is so.

As Cisco defined its "breakaway" differentiation strategy, the company subsequently executed on much of this corporate vision. At each step of the way, Chambers himself was virtually everywhere that a CEO could be telling the Cisco story and how the company sees its future and the future of its industry. While the company was by no means correct all the time, it was correct more than its fair share of the time. The central point here is that the CEO was out on the road, spreading the message. And while Chambers is an excellent communicator, his personal initiative at relaying his corporate message at so many meetings is well worth noting.

As part of a well-managed IR program, the support – and participation – of the company's senior leadership is vital. Chambers was so well traveled and in touch with the financial community, that when he became merely cautious about the company mid-quarter at an analyst conference, which was both Web cast live and picked up by the media reporting the event, many in the investment community made note. Sell-side analysts, including myself, subsequently published various research reports, while some also reduced their earnings estimates. While Cisco didn't officially pre-announce, the message became clear to those that were listening. Chambers was more conservative in his words than usual and that alone was a significant development to those who followed him closely. Cisco's insightful information systems may well have provided its CEO with the information he needed to become cautious. As such, having accurate information and best-in-class information systems remains key to executive decision-making and announcements.

IR programs may take advantage of this softer-approach to managing expectations, so that that major jolts and surprises to the Street can be minimized. By communicating frequently and as early as possible, Chambers seemingly took advantage of his participation at a prearranged sell-side analyst meeting to communicate his concerns.

The Exchange Listed Company's Specialist Firm

If your company's common stock is listed on the New York Stock Exchange, your company's "specialist" is a member of the Exchange. The specialist firm is responsible for maintaining an orderly market in the trading of your NYSE-listed stock on the floor of the exchange. Floor brokers from various brokerage firms, such as Merrill

Lynch and Morgan Stanley, approach the specialist's trading post with orders in hand to buy or sell shares in your company's common stock.

The specialist interacts with traders from sell-side firms such as Morgan Stanley or Goldman Sachs, who are acting in-turn for the clients such as Fidelity or Wellington. The specialist firm may also hold a position in your company's stock in order to maintain a fair and orderly market. In order to maintain an orderly market, the specialist may "stop the stock," allowing the approaching broker to see if he or she can attain a better price in the crowd than what the specialist is offering. If the approaching broker cannot, the specialist agrees to the transaction at the "stop" price. The specialist can never stop trading on a stock, which only an exchange official can do.

The specialist often has interesting insight as to which firms may be purchasing or selling your company's stock. Speaking with the specialist regularly may prove useful to the IRO, as will be visiting the trading post where your company stock is traded. While trading can be done by more automated means, many large Fortune 500 companies remain listed only on the New York Stock Exchange (NYSE).

Listing on the NYSE is one of the most difficult exchange listing for a company to achieve, given its stringent requirements. The listing of company securities on major exchanges, as well as issues traded on the Nasdaq's National Market (NNM), are subject to certain requirement, including minimum revenue, earnings, number of shareholders and maintenance of a minimum share price. Regardless, certain large firms, such as Cisco Systems, have chosen to remain on the NASDAQ instead of moving to the NYSE even though the company would easily qualify for a listing on the big board.

By definition, stocks traded on electronic trading platform do not have a specialist firm responsible for maintaining an orderly market in the trading of the security. Regardless of which exchange or electronic platform that your company is traded on, share transactions will be executed in consistent, fair, and orderly manner. The NYSE is to merge with Archipelago, an electronic trading platform.

Foreign Exchange Listings

I see little benefit to listing on foreign exchanges if you are listed on a major domestic exchange such as the NYSE or the NASDAQ. Most institutional traders will locate shares in your company quite easily if directed to buy shares from the firm's portfolio managers, even if not located on a regional or foreign exchange. In my opinion, the additional expense is not generally beneficial to the company in a quantifiable manner, although some companies prefer multiple exchange listings to aid in their firm's stature as being "multi-local."

The Earnings Blackout Period

Many corporations initiate a "blackout period" which may extend from either the first day of the last month in the quarter or the fifteenth day of the last month in the quarter until the earnings release. During this period of time, companies will generally cease reiterating or otherwise discussing revenue and earnings forecasts for the current quarter, the remainder of the fiscal year or even thereafter. It is prudent for the IRO to remind team members of the initiation of the blackout period each quarter to ensure compliance with the policy.

What The Sell-side Analyst Wants

Frequent Communication

Sell-side analysts interact frequently with institutional investors, marketing their ideas in the aim of generating trading commissions for the firm. While analysts are all different in their personal research styles and their approach to covering their industry sectors, it is generally helpful for them to have frequent dialogue with management and the IRO. By proactively offering a conference call or meeting with members of management, the analyst be greatly appreciative of the effort.

In this way, they are in the loop with respect to the latest commentary available and have more to communicate with their buy-side clients. On earnings day, the sell-side analyst needs dialogue with management or the IRO as soon as possible after the earnings release in order to ask a few clarifying questions, particularly in relation to financial modeling guidance and to assist their understanding of the issues facing the company and industry.

Post-Earnings Clarity

Without clarity on financial modeling, the analyst risks misinterpreting corporate guidance and risks publishing an incorrect financial model. And while no company should "bless" a financial model, many IROs desire an accurate indication of where analyst models are leaning after earnings, especially if they are far apart from the company's internal expectations or external guidance.

Some analysts make names for themselves by taking contrarian viewpoints on the industry or with specific stocks, often by publishing earnings estimates that are significantly above or below corporate guidance. While this may be frustrating for IROs, they should never exert undue influence over or seek to control analyst opinions or viewpoints. At the same time, they have a responsibility to point out facts and issues that may be inaccurate, reiterate official company guidance position. Regardless, the IRO may wind up answering to senior management if an analyst's expectations are highly unrealistic and outside of the norm. The merits of the analysts opinion, as well as those of the company, will play out in due time. In my opinion, contrary opinions need to be respected, for in many respects, they are the fundamental basis for stock trading.

Participation At Sell-side Conferences and Small-group Meetings

Sell-side analysts may sponsor annual industry conferences, at which they invite buy-side analysts and portfolio managers and members of corporate management. By participating in a number of these events, the company can raise its profile in an effective manner, and the analyst can gather an influential group of clients together for a useful day of meetings. The cornerstone of participation is generally large-group presentations that generally draw between one hundred to five hundred individuals. However, most investors attend to hear management further elaborate in breakout rooms or in one-on-one meetings, where questions can be asked more comfortably.

Sell-side analysts often seek to bring a small group of select institutional clients together for lunch or dinner with a member of senior management. While it is easy enough for the IRO to coordinate such a meeting independently, it is generally acceptable for IROs to take advantage of such offers occasionally. As with all investor communications, care should be taken not to offer material information to a select group of investors.

Don't Retrench The IR Program In Challenging Times

The communications process that IR employs must be designed to effectively market the company over the long term, and never to maximize dialogue in the good times and minimize it in the more difficult times. Investor communication programs are equally as important in the difficult times as they are in the good times, although there is a natural tendency for IR programs to expand in the good times and contract in the challenging ones. Truly best in class IR programs accelerate their meetings program in more challenging times.

By retrenching an IR program, the company may believe that doing so is the conservative approach. The predominant theory may be that a lack of communication can't make the situation worse. Unfortunately, it can't make the situation better either. Indeed, the preferred approach is to *increase* IR communication efforts and travel markedly in order to maintain and develop the company's credibility at communication the most recent facts.

Markedly Increase Communication During Challenging Periods

As an investor, if you have sufficient access to the company in bad times, as well as the good, you will consistently receive answers to hard questions even if the answers involve various industry or company-specific concerns. Regardless, by providing such an understanding, a number of investors will give your management team high marks for making the effort, even if they chose to stay on the sidelines for now. Investors are usually receptive to company offers to meet and discuss issues.

UNDERSTANDING INVESTOR RELATIONS

In my opinion, a company's stock can be impacted by both negative financial results and by having investors feeling uninformed. By offering less access to senior management than desired, some may develop negative perceptions of the company and even the integrity of the company and its management. There is likely no greater issue for investors than corporate integrity, and we only need to look back at the Enron/Arthur Anderson scandals of 2000 to be reminded of the importance of corporate integrity. On August 14, 2002, new rules were established whereby corporate officers were required to certify the integrity of their financial statements.

As a member of management, you should look your investors in the eye during bad times and give them bad news. It is important to outline your observations of the issues facing the company and the market, as well as the specific steps you are taking to address them. Investors need to see your roadmap at every step of the way, and by sharing as much of the roadmap that you can, they will better understand the complex issues facing your company and how you intend to manage through them. They will most likely hold management accountable to update them on progress toward goals.

Accordingly, it is strongly encouraged that all IROs and management teams not to retrench their communications efforts, but to seek to *increase* them. We reiterate that helping the investment community better understand your company and its place in a changing industry should be embraced as a primary goal. It is not enough for management to shelter themselves from criticism and questions, it is far better to communicate frequently in bad times than to leave the investment community assuming the worst.

We acknowledge that many CEOs and CFOs need to devote their attentions to leading their corporate restructuring efforts and that those efforts are critical to once-again being viewed in a positive light. However, the needs of the investment community must not be overlooked. It is important for members of management to realize that they need not hold off on their interactions with the financial community until restructuring details finalize, but rather simply communicate progress and issues.

Reaching Out of The IR Box

It is strongly encouraged for members of the IR team to reach out and meet individuals inside and outside the company. There may be quite a number of engineers, esteemed scientists, external financial analysts and investors that can provide the IRO with different, and useful, perspectives.

As such, it is often very beneficial to go beyond the normal finance and public relations channels and venture into the company's research and development (R&D) community and even touring manufacturing facilities. Similarly, by discussing the industry with corporate marking teams conducting competitor intelligence and business development, will give the IRO a broader sense of the company and provide an intuitive place in the broader industry.

Meeting with many people both inside and outside the company can be quite beneficial as the IRO becomes an especially valued member and trusted advisor to senior management.

Remain Focused

In meetings with the investment community, it is important that executives and IROs remain keenly focused on furthering their understanding the company, competitive environment and other important areas of interest. Such areas include understanding regulatory issues that can radically change market dynamics or the rate of technology adoption. Care should be taken to avoid commentary on sensitive areas such as discussion on specific company relationships with various component suppliers, distributors or potential acquisition candidates. Many investors will ask very specific questions about smaller suppliers in order to learn insights into how your business is expected to moderate up or down in the future, or which technologies your technical programs will employ.

Many investors will ask probing questions about various relationships in an effort to gain insight on alternative investments or shorting activities. Large public companies often make significant revenue contributions to their component suppliers and they can make or break them by strategically moving business toward them or away from them.

Provide Management Feedback, Executive Updates and Voice Mail

Periodically, management should receive e-mails from the IRO, informing senior management of recent events that may be influencing both the broader stock market and the trading of the company's stock. Accordingly, such items as "Corporate Market Updates" can become a routine part of the weekly work product of the IR team. These updates can help senior management stay informed of major industry developments and analyst research reports. Such updates are not to be intended for the entire employee base, but rather should be focused on senior management and their needs.

Similarly, after the company's quarterly earnings releases, e-mail updates should follow with market commentary and analyst research alike. Additionally, e-mail updates should generally provide management with analyst notes that follow the quarterly earnings releases and large-group meetings of the company's major competitors. In this way, e-mail updates will help management stay further informed of the results of their competitors and the ongoing concerns and opinions of sell-side research analysts.

When your management meets with sell-side analysts, it is also desirable to forward any resulting analyst notes.

Corporate Media Training

Along with members of senior management, it is highly recommended that members of the IR and PR teams receive corporate media training. Any external spokesperson having extensive contact with the investment community and media can benefit from this training. While the experience of going through a media training program will not accurately reflect dealing with the media or investment community in most circumstances, it is important to learn a few of the basics approaches that can be drawn upon when dealing with either analysts or the media alike. With both members of the media and investment community alike, in my opinion comments should always be considered on the record. As a general and helpful rule, corporate spokespersons should not venture commentary in an issue that they would not want seen on the front page of the Wall Street Journal.

Corporate media training programs often include placing the management trainee in front of a camera for a spontaneous sit-down interview, confronted with various questions about the industry and company's history, such as distant acquisitions and earnings details. The questions asked can be so difficult in nature that the IRO in training has but few answers at hand.

While the trainee may not be aware of it, the camera may even be rolling upon initial introductions with their trainer. In such way, the IRO learns that *everything* is on the record, even under the most casual of circumstances. Other major lessons that often result from the training include not trying to answer a question when you really don't know the answer, something that many try to do. After all, the individuals in training after all are supposed to have the answers!

While initial commentary and spin ventured forth by the IRO can sometimes avoid the difficult question sufficiently, detailed follow-up questions often reveal the true lack of knowledge. By replaying taped video segments of the interview back, the dialogue often shows the various pauses, stutters and glances at either peers or the interviewer. Naturally, most real interviews are not nearly as difficult as media training portends and answers can be offered with much more ease and relaxation.

Other media training techniques including playing videotapes of interviews with well-spoken individuals such as Teddy Roosevelt, Ronald Reagan, or Britain's Queen Elizabeth and Winston Churchill. Listening carefully to their responses to difficult questions leads to identifying some clever and skillful responses. The lessons of media training are few but valuable, and the experience will most certainly remain with the participant for years to come. While not inexpensive, the experience and coaching will be worth the time and effort.

With time, your interaction with certain individuals will most certainly reveal which analysts and media generally seek sensational and headline grabbing commentary. It is important to remember that some individual reporters or analysts will be in the midst of highly detailed research and may be seeking corporate commentary and data that supports their initial conclusions.

Proactive Initiatives

Investor Relations programs should be managed with a watchful eye toward monitoring the volume of meetings conducted in a proactive manner versus on a request basis. Simply being aware of the ratio is an important aspect of managing an effective program. If the company is conducting a high percentage of meetings due to specific requests, it is likely to be planning too few group events and conference calls, while managing too many specific requests for one-on-one meetings. Accordingly, such IR programs will be resource constrained and will not be using management time as wisely as possible.

If managed correctly, no more than half of the meetings conducted by the IR team will be on a request basis. With a proactive IR meetings program in place, the company will reach ample groups of investors, limiting the need for many specific meeting requests. While it is critical that topics of interest be addressed in a timely manner, it is also important that the company's IR program be highly proactive and use management time wisely.

Given extremely limited resources, many IR programs are only able to conduct a few large group meetings per year and manage only a limited numbers of analyst and investor interactions. In these instances, the creation of a detailed IR marketing plan may be useful to generating management support for an expanded IR program and driving additional attention and interest in the stock.

Outsourcing Investor Relations

Clearly, many smaller companies tend to outsource the entire function of Investor Relations to strategic partners while larger ones tend to have IR programs managed by dedicated line employees. Additionally, many large companies utilize IR consultants to assist with strategic issues, developing meetings plans, cultivating new analyst coverage and assisting with logistical arrangements. Still others have external assistance in tracking institutional shareholders by engaging the services of stock surveillance firms and by commissioning external benchmarking studies.

While Investor Relations programs can be effectively managed by either dedicated internal employees or external outsourcing partners alike, senior management must oversee these programs to ensure that they are both sufficiently active and exceeding shareholders' expectations. Simply tasking an external IR agency to respond to investor inquiries and distribute corporate press releases is far from managing an effective and proactive IR program. If a company chooses to outsource its IR activities, having sufficient management and IRO oversight is critical.

Investor "Perception Studies" and Benchmarking

Annual investor "perception studies" are often useful at providing management and the IRO with direct feedback from the investment community on a variety of important issues. By conducting in-depth telephone interviews with the buy-side and sell-side, candid "blind" feedback in the form of an investor perception study can be quite insightful. Feedback is typically generated on issues ranging from investor understanding of the company's strategy, product portfolio and gaps, strength of management, the Investor Relations program and even the effectiveness of the IRO. There are many useful insights that can be provided to senior management by conducting these surveys. Perception studies are generally conducted by external consultants, including the company's stock surveillance firm or survey consultant and often include separate executive summaries that are intended for use by senior management.

Marketing To Non-U.S. Investors

While U.S.-based money managers and individual investors will hold the far majority of equity in most U.S. public companies, there are occasions when marketing to international fund managers is highly appropriate. Marketing outside the United States is often not practical for other than larger Fortune companies. Those that seek to attract the attention of the international investment community usually seek to do so by conducting extensive road shows within Europe or Asia.

Reaching the European financial community can be adequately achieved by hosting meetings in the major European financial centers, principally London, Geneva, Zurich and Paris. Historically, while many European investors have tended to invest in more value-oriented stocks as opposed to aggressive growth stocks, given the conservative nature of the European investor base, there is generally a willingness to hear an interesting and compelling story. Regardless, when spreadsheets are run on the holdings of even the largest European funds, their share holdings in a particular U.S. stock will likely be relatively small.

Marketing to European fund managers will certainly provide management with a better sense of the long-term and macro concerns which exist for the company and industry. The European investor base is significantly different than its U.S. counterpart and will likely surprise management by the commendable long-term bias and low-turnover characteristic of European investors. By and large, these investors are not looking for short-term profits and are most interested in market fundamentals as opposed to focusing on particular short-term earnings results and contract announcements. The day-to-day issues that Wall Street spends countless hours analyzing and making speculative "calls," are often of significantly less interest to European investors.

Likewise, visiting the major financial centers of Asia, and in particular Japan, China and Singapore will be very beneficial to management as well. Coordinating meetings in major international financial institutions generally requires local knowledge about venue selection, first-hand knowledge of the major local financial institutions and the customs of local money managers. If it has a good international skill-set, the company's stock surveillance firm is capable of prioritizing candidates for one-on-one meetings and for participation at group luncheon or breakfast meetings. The search for investment returns is indeed global in nature, perhaps now more than ever before.

IR Awards

By submitting a summary of the company's extensive IR program for various awards, the IRO can gain significant external recognition for its ongoing communications efforts. The company's public relations team can likely suggest some industry awards for submission, including the Golden Quill PR award. Others include the likes of Institutional Investor magazine and other IR-specific rankings. Often many categories exist, such as Best Investor Relations for an IPO and even for the best Investor Relations Officers (IROs). Many organizations issue Investor Relations awards based on market capitalization, so that resource-constrained small and mid cap companies receive their fair share of program recognition.

Top Shareholder Recognition Events

Companies can chose to recognize their largest institutional or retail shareholders in various creative ways. As an example, by sponsoring a reception and dinner meeting with just one invitee from each of the company's top ten or fifteen shareholders, members of senior management can extend a personal acknowledgements for their investing confidence in the company.

The Earnings Announcement

There are many logistical issues that must be managed during the quarterly book-close process and blackout period. There are many strategic and legal disclosure issues that must be made durning the book-close process, depending on the level of complexity of the quarter. These issues can include the number of acquisitions made, a variety of one-time items, whether or not to report book and/or pro-forma results, and in what format. An earnings report is not usually as detailed as a SEC Form 10Q or 10K which typically follows the corporate earnings announcement. The SEC documents will generally be completed by the Controller/External Reporting and Legal teams.

Many companies report earnings results on a typical schedule, such as ten or twenty days after the close of the quarter, depending on the complexity of the book-close and consolidation processes. As an IR team, characterization of overall results of products and regions depends on the level of disclosure that the company is comfortable with. Every company has its own format, but once a precedent of disclosing more information, it may be difficult to report results without such level of detail.

Corporate revenue discussions during a quarterly earnings announcement are often made with either highly specific percentage or dollar changes, or broader statements, such as:

> "Sales increased 10.1 percent for the quarter in comparison to the year-ago period, led by a 13.3 percent increase in product line A, 9.8 percent increase in product line B, and 3.1 percent increase in product line C. Sales increased 12.1 percent in North America, 7.3 percent in the Asia/Pacific region, with a decline in 2.1 percent in Latin America."

> "Sales increased 10.1 percent for the quarter in comparison to the year-ago period, led by increases in product line A, product line B, and product line C. Sales increased in North America, Asia Pacific, with a decline in Latin America."

Other corporations prefer the use of qualifiers to results such as "strong," "good," and "fair." Companies which use such qualifiers may have internal meaning to them, such as:

> "Strong" equating to increases of in excess of twenty-percent;
> "Very Good" equating to increases of ten- to twenty-percent;
> "Good" equating to increases of five- to ten-percent;
> "Fair" equating to increases of zero to five-percent;

Given that such meaning may be less than understood, it may be best to avoid such qualifiers and discuss overall results either highly specifically or with broader statements. While the IR team is working the strategic and logistical elements of preparing for quarterly earnings announcement, the normal day to day issues of planning for meetings and conferences continue during the blackout period.

10

Logistical Elements of Investor Relations

The Book-Close Process and Quarterly Earnings Process

Managing the quarterly earnings process is indeed complex at most large companies. To help frame the detailed timetable of the events surrounding the earnings process, creating a detailed earnings calendar is very useful. In this way, a helpful list of planned meetings, conference calls and deliverable due dates for draft and final versions of the corporate earnings release, conference call script, question and answer document and talking points will help guide their creation. Developing a detailed earnings calendar and distributed it in advance of earnings will help set the stage for good logistical coordination between all members of the working team. The earnings calendar will likely be distributed to members of the IR team, as well as the legal, public relations and finance communities – likely including CEO, CFO, Treasurer, Controller, Corporate Secretary and Public Relations Officer.

Additionally, as the IR program manager is tasked with managing administrative functions for the team, developing a specific "check list" of earnings day responsibilities will assist the program manager in the coordination of various tasks. These tasks often include loading the press release or earnings bulletins onto First Call the day before distribution, coordinating conference call and Web cast logistics, disseminating copies of final materials and conference call scripts to executives and distributing analyst "call back lists" to line members of the IR team. The program manager will also ensuring that e-mail and fax lists are ready for distribution. Members of the retail team will often ensure that the corporate Web site has the latest earnings press release, conference call details and associated presentation materials.

Control "Hyper-driven" IR Programs With "Meetings Meetings" and The Eighteen-Month Investor Relations Calendar

Reviewing the most recent planning status of all IR activities with periodic "meetings meetings" will ensure that modification to existing plans and decisions are made expeditiously and that effective controls are being placed on IR activities. Accordingly, the IRO will meet often to review various meetings requests, discuss calendar conflicts and decide which IR resources best support planned activities.

The meetings are a great venue to review high-level details of the large group analyst meeting, road shows and activities at trade shows and other industry venues. The IRO will also review executive availability and select suitable executives for participation at various conferences and other initiatives. Modifications to corporate messages, themes and presentation materials for external conferences can be discussed, as well as coordinating public relations announcements and coordinating the overall activities of the IR effort. Further, individual IR team members will be tasked with ownership of particular IR activities and will provide periodic updates on progress or issues being faced, and potentially requiring IRO intervention.

In this way, the IR plan will uniquely adapt itself to the company's ongoing requests for meetings and events participation, while at the same time maintaining the cornerstones of its annual plan. The planning of "meetings meetings" may follow general IR staff meetings, with only those involved specifically in the meetings program remaining behind for participation. Holding such meetings every two weeks is likely sufficient.

Among items distributed at "meetings meetings" will likely include a spreadsheet showing eighteen-months worth of IR activities. This calendar is particularly useful at framing the broader Investor Relations program and seeing natural calendar conflicts. Other items that will likely be discussed at the "meetings meetings" include lists of future executive availability, upcoming executive travel schedules and a database of IR activities previously supported sorted both by executive and participant. In this way, ample checks and balances can be placed on the program.

Secure Time On Management Calendars In Advance

To coordinate management participation at so many events, securing time slots on executive calendars for indeterminate "investor events' well in advance of the dates that meeting details are determined is highly recommend. In this way, IROs can chose to utilize or release those time slots based on meeting demand and company issues. Also, establishing a monthly process to collect data on executive availability and travel schedules via email request is highly helpful. Over time, those time slots will establish a framework for ensuring that the most important meetings occur, including regional management road shows.

Investor Relations Marketing Materials

For almost every one-on-one and small-group meeting, the IRO will generally need an up-to-date package of materials to be given to visiting members of the financial community. At such meetings, it is important never to meet with investors empty-handed since the materials may be necessary to facilitate discussion of the company and its industry. These take-away materials also act as effective plane reading material, as well as good reference materials for portfolio managers. For the purpose of hosting small group meetings, members of the company's IR team are best suited to preparing most of these packages.

Perhaps the most important of the documents contained in the investor package is an effective and up-to-date company presentation. It is important that the presentation be new and informative, and not used for too long a period of time without being refreshed with new messages and information. While the presentation must convey new material, it must also reinforce overall corporate themes, consistently, so that the material is not entirely foreign to the listener. The large presentations are often prepared by the company's public relations team and are tailored to areas of investor interest.

It is important that for most meetings hosted by the IR team, that they have presentation material available *if needed*. At some meetings, investors and analysts will come very well prepared and have more questions than you will answer. For these meetings, the presentation package will become a take-away. For others however, the presentation will be a critical element to the meeting, for without the structure that the presentation provides, visitors may not receive a broad and thorough overview of the company. The full investor package may contain recent press releases, a product catalog, 10Ks/ 10Qs, recent quarterly earnings reports and the most recent annual report.

Corporate Subject Matter Experts (SMEs)

Members of senior management will likely become highly reliable partners in executing the IR plan. While the company's CFO will likely be chief spokesperson to the investment community, it is strongly encouraged that the IRO develop a broad list of talented and well spoken subject matter experts that can be relied upon to represent the company at various levels of detail to members of the financial community. By utilizing additional executives outside of the CFO, CEO and other senior executives, the IRO can draw from a deep pool of talent for IR activities.

By developing a deep pool of talent, investors and analysts will come to realize the depth of the company's talent and will likely understand more about it from technical or operational perspectives than they otherwise would. Logistically, by developing a database or spreadsheet of available subject matter experts, their locations, secretaries, and contact information, the IR administrative staff will have easier access to executive and subject matter expert (SME) calendars and availability.

Executive Briefing Letters and Packages

In advance of analyst visits, management road shows, or major trade show events, it is important to prepare corporate executives for upcoming meetings by providing detailed meeting schedules and itineraries, institutional profiles on buy-side firms in attendance and recent First Call research notes on the company from attending sell-side analysts. For group meetings, it is useful to provide management with the collective shareholdings of meeting participants as well as their collective purchase potential of additional shares.

Executive briefing packages should also contain copies of recent corporate press releases, quarterly earnings documents, and the most recent public relations question and answer document. For one-on-one meetings, a simple briefing letter with confirmation of meeting logistics and analyst profiles may be sufficient. It is also worthwhile to note any previous meetings that have been recently scheduled so that senior management is aware of such interactions.

Any specific areas of interest on the minds of meeting participants should be learned in advance of the meeting and given to management to help focus their thoughts in advance. Arranging fifteen minutes on executive calendars in advance of one-on-one conference calls is often sufficient to cover any last minutes issues.

Executive Secretaries, Members of Your Extended Team

Having a spreadsheet of detailed executive contact information for executives and their secretaries will be most useful. When scheduling meetings, IR interactions will often be with executive secretaries that often control their officers' calendars. Accordingly, establishing good relationships with executive secretaries will be key to having their support for your program. To show IRO appreciation for their ongoing efforts in supporting the IR program, it is advisable to consider hosting a secretaries' luncheon to provide them with an understanding of Wall Street, the key elements of the IR plan and to thank them for supporting your aggressive program.

While the IR program manager and administrative team can host this meeting on a peer level, it is desirable for the IRO to meet the group and to answer any questions that they may have about the IR program. By doing so, the extended members of your IR team will better understand the need for time on their executives' calendars and can be a truly valued and supportive aspect of the IR team. The executive secretaries will be very grateful for your thinking of them and for appreciating their help in ascertaining time on executive calendars. Tiffany's stationary is likely to be a well-received gift.

Constant Availability, Cell Phone and Wireless E-mail PDAs

IROs generally make themselves available on a nearly 24x7 basis, checking their voice mail and answering questions from the investment community. Many IROs would rather be available, even on weekends, rather than have misunderstandings and unsubstantiated rumors circulate and persist with analysts and investors. They are wise to carry a wireless e-mail PDA and leave their cell phones on. Late on a Sunday afternoon, an analyst may find herself seriously rethinking stock ratings, earnings estimates or price targets. There are occasions, although certainly not always, when analysts seek input from the IRO before making substantial adjustments to public positions on the company or the sector. Should the analyst get the compulsion to alter her rating first thing on Monday morning, she might well desire some final thoughts from the IRO before pulling the trigger on the First Call note. Be available at all times to provide any assistance and to inform senior management, if necessary.

Important Disclaimer

This text contains the opinions of the author and should not be relied upon or considered as representing fact. It contains background information only. You should carefully review any statements made, including consulting your own legal, regulatory, investment or tax advisors as necessary. Any aspect of legal requirements or interpretations of regulations and practices that may or may not be required of public or private companies, including but not limited to disclosure rules and other legal matters, should be discussed with legal, regulatory, tax or financial counsel as necessary. The material is not intended as advice or recommendation. Neither author or other associated entity makes any claim or warranty about legal, regulatory or other requirements, including but not limited to those regarding corporate communications, investor relations, public relations or other areas that may be referenced, discussed, suggested, or otherwise directly or indirectly referenced in this document. Neither the author nor other associated entity makes any claim or warranty whatsoever, nor shall be liable for any losses, damages, costs or expenses, of any kind or description, relating to the adequacy, accuracy or completeness of this material, nor do they have any obligation to update you of any changes that may occur in the future that may impact the material and subject content. No warranty either express or otherwise is provided. Any written material provided to you in this document is not intended to offer legal or investment advice or counsel to the reader. Certain information contained in this material constitutes "forward-looking statements," which can be identified by the use of forward-looking terminology such as "may," "will," "should," or "believe," or the negatives thereof or other variations thereon or comparable terminology.

Printed in Great Britain
by Amazon.co.uk, Ltd.,
Marston Gate.